German Resistance to Hitler

Hitler's headquarters "Wolfschanze," before midday situation briefing, 15 July 1944. From left: Colonel Claus Count von Stauffenberg, Rear Admiral Karl Jesko von Puttkamer, General Karl Bodenschatz, Hitler, Fieldmarshal Wilhelm Keitel.

German Resistance to Hitler

Peter Hoffmann

Harvard University Press
Cambridge, Massachusetts
London, England

Library of Congress Cataloging-in-Publication Data
Hoffmann, Peter, 1930–
  German resistance to Hitler.
  Originally published in German under title:
Widerstand gegen Hitler.
  Bibliography: p.
  Includes index.
  1. Anti-Nazi movement.   2. Hitler, Adolf, 1889–1945—
Assassination attempt, 1944 (July 20)   I. Title.
DD256.3.H59513   1988   943.086'092'4   87-15038
ISBN 0-674-35085-5 (alk. paper)
ISBN 0-674-35086-3 (pbk. : alk. paper)

For P.F. and S.J.

Preface

This book examines German opposition to Hitler's dictatorship. It deals with the stages of recognition of the regime's evil nature in Germany, the degrees of entanglement with it, and the levels of commitment against it.

An earlier, shorter version of the study appeared in German under the title *Widerstand gegen Hitler: Probleme des Umsturzes* (Munich, Zurich: R. Piper & Co. Verlag, 1979). The present study has been wholly rewritten and much expanded.

Permission to quote from published works is acknowledged gratefully to Don Congdon Associates, Inc., for a passage from William L. Shirer, *Berlin Diary,* and to Macmillan Publishing Co. for a passage from Albert Speer, *Inside the Third Reich.*

For help with research, I thank the staffs of the McLennan Library, McGill University, Montreal; Württembergische Landesbibliothek, Stuttgart; Bibliothek für Zeitgeschichte, Stuttgart; Institut für Zeitgeschichte, Munich; Bundesarchiv in Koblenz and Freiburg i.Br.; and Politisches Archiv, Auswärtiges Amt, Bonn. I am grateful to the Faculty of Graduate Studies and Research in McGill University and to the Social Sciences and Humanities Research Council of Canada for their support. I thank my colleague Robert Vogel for his incisive suggestions on the manuscript, and my editor, Virginia LaPlante, for her labors. My deepest gratitude belongs to my father, the late Dr. Wilhelm Hoffmann, who commented on my work with kind and uncompromising criticism.

Contents

German Resistance to Hitler

Introduction

More than four decades after the end of the Nazi era, interest in the events of the time remains high. Western society continues to try to comprehend the nature and dimensions of the evil that emanated from Hitler and the Third Reich.

Most Germans had no more than fragmentary knowledge of Hitler's crimes. Those who were not his accomplices in the crimes rarely understood their general outlines, to say nothing of their full dimensions. Even those, both inside and outside Germany, who opposed the Nazi government did not have full information about the mass extermination of Jews, Gypsies, Poles, Communists, the mentally ill, and Russian prisoners of war. Yet the limited information about those crimes available to Germans revealed such a monstrous menace to the country and to humanity that it shook a number of Germans to the depths of their being and drove them into anti-Nazi activities at the risk of their lives.

The fact that thousands of Germans resisted the crimes of their government has been an embarrassment to the millions who supported Hitler. Little is said in German schools today about the Resistance in the Nazi era, so that the general public has little knowledge about the Resistance. Polls taken of representative population samples in the Federal Republic of Germany in April 1970 and April 1984 revealed that, among those 16 to 29 years old in 1970, 47 percent could not cite any fact about the attempt to overthrow Hitler on 20 July 1944. In 1984, this figure had increased to 63 percent. Fifty-one percent of the same age group in 1970 could not give the name of any person in the German Resistance. Of those in all age groups in both years who knew anything about the coup attempt of 20 July 1944, about 35 percent could not give the name of a single leading figure in the Resistance. Among those 16 to 19 years old who knew anything of the events of 20 July 1944, 66 percent in 1970 and 55 percent in 1984 could produce the name of the intended assassin, Colonel Claus Count von Stauffenberg; 13 percent and 8 percent respectively knew the name of the presumptive head of government, Carl Goerdeler; 8 percent and 5 percent respectively knew the name of the presumptive head of state, General Ludwig Beck; and 2 percent and 4 percent respectively knew the name of the presumptive commander in chief of the Armed Forces, Fieldmarshal Erwin von Witzleben. Only 14 percent in this age group in 1970, and 7 percent in 1984, could refer correctly to clergymen, trade unionists, socialists, and Communists in the Resistance.[1]

There is considerable disagreement, in Germany and elsewhere, as to whether internal opposition to Hitler's regime was treason or an ethical imperative. In Hitler's dictatorship, the laws expressing the ethical and legal concepts of Western civilization had been perverted to suit his despotic rule. Socially approved behavior and law conflicted with the values of Judeo-Christian culture. The conflict between law and the perceived true interests of the nation required a decision for or against the government. Since many people gave their lives on one or the other side of this issue, strong emotions are still involved.

The German opposition to the Nazi regime began to be assessed almost immediately after the war, although the Allied occupation authorities discouraged interest in the subject.[2] Memoirs, letters, biographies, and other historical works started to appear, first in Switzerland, Britain, and America, and since 1949, in the Federal Republic of Germany (the western German state). These materials laid the foundation for reevaluating the Resistance as a revolt of conscience. At the same time, the camp of unreformed Nazis released a flood of apologetic literature, declaring that Hitler's German enemies had been traitors. In the eastern German state, called the German Democratic Republic, the Resistance of the political Left alone was regarded as legitimate until 1964, when a book was published by a Soviet Russian writer on the conspiracy of 20 July 1944, the major military attempt to overthrow Hitler.[3]

The Parliamentary Council which in 1948 and 1949 wrote the Constitution of the Federal Republic of Germany incorporated some of the ideas of the Resistance. A few survivors of the Resistance played a role in postwar politics, the most prominent being Kurt Schumacher of the Social Democratic Party (SPD) and Eugen Gerstenmaier and Jakob Kaiser of the Christian Democratic Union (CDU). From 1952 onward the Federal Republic, under the control of the CDU and the Christian Social Union (CSU), regularly published official statements to commemorate the uprising of 20 July 1944. In 1954 the President of the Federal Republic, Theodor Heuss, remarked in a public speech that the legacy of the Resistance had not yet been acknowledged.[4] Earnest efforts to do so followed. The Armed Forces honored the imperative of conscience by naming a number of Armed Forces installations after prominent Resistance figures, such as Lieutenant Colonel Eberhard Finckh and Stauffenberg.

The Nazi crimes, and the battle waged against them by a few within Nazi Germany, challenge all human beings to comprehend the nature of tyranny. Hitler's rule cannot be understood without a grasp of the resistance to Nazi crimes, for the very nature of the Third Reich evoked the most uncompromising opposition as well as the enthusiasm of the masses. The relation between National Socialism and the Resistance is a key to comprehending the Nazi system.

Part One

The Rise of Hitler

Path to Dictatorship 1

The Weimar Republic is widely held synonymous with liberty and emancipation, a flourishing of the arts, republicanism, and reform of the German soul after its aberration under a "Prussian Hohenzollern" emperor. So much of German tradition that was good—the music, literature, philosophy, university system, and the revolutionary goals of 1848—had apparently been disrupted by the Bismarckian Prusso-German Empire. In the years after 1918, the good traditions seemed to come into their own again. The National Assembly of 1919 stressed this revival by meeting in the classical city of German literature, Weimar. The seeds of the new had been Cubism and Expressionism in the visual arts, Expressionism in poetry and prose, and radical Socialism in politics. The Republic that emerged was democratic, liberal, and pluralistic; it offered political emancipation and intellectual and artistic vitality.

But the Republic was burdened with the legacy of the Great War: defeat, humiliation, and loss of territory and of German-speaking populations. Many Germans believed that those now in the Weimar government had helped to bring about the defeat, that it had been a stab in the back. The Treaty of Versailles had forced Germany to accept sole responsibility for the war and to surrender immediately 13.5 percent of its territory, including over 10 percent of its population (seven million citizens), 75 percent of its iron-ore deposits, its entire Navy, and all merchantmen over 1,600 tons gross and half of those 1,000 tons gross and over. The old German provinces of West Prussia,

Upper Silesia, and Alsace-Lorraine were lost; the Austrian Germans in Bohemia (Sudeten) were forced into Czechoslovakia; and rump-Austria was forbidden by the Allies to unite its territory with Germany, although both parliaments had voted for the union. Germany had to limit its Army to 100,000 men and surrender most of its artillery. Inside its borders Germany had to clear a deep zone of fortifications. Germany could not station troops on German soil west of the Rhine nor in a specified zone about twenty miles east of the Rhine; it had to accept foreign military occupation of the western Rhine region and of part of the eastern Rhine region. Germany could not maintain a tank force or an air force. Germany had to surrender goods in vast quantities and sign over future commercial opportunities. Any private German assets abroad were confiscated against reparations demands, and delivery of reparations payments in kind and in currency had to begin immediately. Germany had to agree, by signing the treaty on 28 June 1919, to meet whatever reparations demands would be imposed in future. Germany would not be informed of the total amount until January 1921. The impositions were astronomical, and according to the British economist John Maynard Keynes, they were wholly unrealistic—unless they had been designed as incapable of fulfillment.[1]

German governments attempted to meet the demands. They adopted a "fulfillment policy," for the purpose of demonstrating the unreasonableness of the demands and getting them modified. But the policy failed because it was not meant to succeed. When German payments were in arrears to the extent of 37,583 meters of sawn lumber and 98,867 meters of telegraph poles in December 1922, the governments of France, Belgium, and Italy—with Britain voting against the majority—determined that Germany was in "voluntary default."[2] In January 1923 French and other foreign troops occupied and appropriated the heart of German industry in the Ruhr region. Having been disarmed under the Treaty of Versailles, Germany could not defend itself. Its economy and currency collapsed, causing millions to lose their life savings through devaluation. In July 1923 an American dollar was worth 353,412 marks; in August, 4,620,455 marks; and in October, 25 billion marks. On 15 November 1923, the day of the introduction of a new German currency, one American dollar cost 4 trillion marks.[3] At the same time, there was unrest and sedition. The French government sponsored separatist movements in the Rhine region and in Bavaria. Left-wing and right-wing conspiracies and putsches were aimed, respectively, at turning the Republic into a soviet or a fascist dictatorship.

Right-wing extremists had demanded in 1919 that the German government refuse to sign the Treaty of Versailles. This would have led to the occupation of Germany. The government offered to resign and to let the right-wing parties assume responsibility, but these declined, preferring to continue agitating against the Republic, branding its governments traitors to the nation. The right-wing extremists claimed that they knew how to restore German independence, honor, and greatness: through dictatorship, rearmament, and reconquest. At the polls, appeals against "Versailles," against the "fulfillment politicians," and against the "criminals" of 1918 who had formed the Republic always found support—considerably more support, in fact, than the crude anti-Semitism of certain right-wing orators.

When the economy collapsed in the Great Depression of 1929, the right-wing extremists again received increased voter support. Unemployment, business failures, and internal conflicts raised the specter of a Communist-Bolshevik takeover. There were riots, local insurrections, pitched battles between revolutionaries and police and army units, strikes, and widespread misery among the unemployed. The political party most successful in taking advantage of the conditions was the National Socialist German Workers' Party (NSDAP, Nazi Party). The extreme Left, the Communist Party, increased its support only gradually, from 12.6 percent of the popular vote in 1924 to 16.9 percent in November 1932. In the same period the Social Democrats' share of the vote rose from 20.5 percent in 1924 to 29.8 percent in 1928, dropping back to 20.4 percent in November 1932. But the Nazi Party was catapulted to national importance in the Reichstag elections of September 1930. After receiving 6.6 percent of the popular vote, or 32 Reichstag seats, in May 1924, the Nazis had won only 2.6 percent of the popular vote, or 12 Reichstag seats, in the elections of May 1928. In September 1930, they increased their support to 18.3 percent, for 107 Reichstag seats.[4]

In the economic crisis, voter turnout increased from over 75 percent through the 1920s to over 80 percent in the elections from 1930 to 1933. But extremism was also growing, at both ends of the political spectrum. In the presidential elections of March 1932, Hitler's candidacy forced President von Hindenburg, at eighty-four years of age, to stand again, although he had hoped to retire. He declared that he was a candidate in order to prevent the election of "a partisan politician who represented one-sided and extreme interests." Hindenburg missed the required absolute majority by 0.5 percent, Hitler received 30.1 percent of the votes, followed by the Communist Party leader Ernst Thälmann with 13 percent and the German National People's Party's candidate, Theodor Duesterberg, with 6.8 percent. In the run-off election in April 1932, Duesterberg did not run again, and Hindenburg received 53 percent of the votes, but Hitler increased his support to 36.8 percent, followed by Thälmann with 10.2 percent.[5] This ratio more or less continued through 1932. In the Reichstag elections in July 1932, the Nazis received 37.4 percent of the votes; their share declined to 33.1 percent by November. Two-thirds of the voters rejected Hitler and his party; but almost 50 percent of all voters supported the two extremist parties.

In 1932 there were nine political parties in the Weimar Republic drawing 1 percent each or more of the popular vote. The highest vote percentages in either of the two Reichstag elections of 1932 were achieved by four parties: the NSDAP, up to 37.4 percent; the SPD, up to 20.6 percent; the Communist Party of Germany (Kommunistische Partei Deutschlands, or KPD), up to 16.9 percent; and the Center Party, up to 12.5 percent. The German National People's Party (Deutschnationale Volkspartei, or DNVP) drew between 5.9 percent and 8.9 percent. One other party received more than 1.2 percent, namely the German-Hanoverian Party, receiving 3.2 percent and 3.1 percent respectively in the two Reichstag elections of 1932.

These figures indicate the possibilities and impossibilities of forming coalitions. Majority support in the Reichstag was necessary to form a regular parliamentary government. Since no single party ever received anything close to 50 percent of the popular vote, majority governments were composed of varying party coalitions. The radicalization of politics led to the situation that several of the moderate parties or the radical parties had to form a coalition in order to secure the support of a majority of Reichstag deputies. When neither of these possibilities materialized, the Constitution gave the Reich President authority to appoint an emergency government.

Such an event occurred in March 1930. In order to govern—that is, to adopt a budget and enact other essential legislation—the minority government of Chancellor Heinrich Brüning undertook the constitutionally proper expedient of issuing emergency decrees authorized by President von Hindenburg.[6] Although Brüning governed within the bounds of legality and did his best to contain and control Nazi and Communist extremism, the fact is that from this date a constitutionally legal dictatorship existed under presidential authority. This had some bearing on the public attitude when, after two more Chancellors had been appointed under the presidential emergency power, Hitler's turn came.

Another pattern-setting series of circumstances surrounded Brüning's fall from power. In May 1932 Hindenburg suddenly dismissed Brüning and replaced him with Franz von Papen.[7] There was no constitutional reason for Brüning's dismissal. It was brought about by intrigue, and all the steps leading to it were taken in secrecy and haste, so that if the Reichstag had wanted to keep Brüning in power by a majority vote of confidence, it had no opportunity to do so. Although the President was well intentioned, his age had taken its toll, and he passed increasingly under the influence of private, irresponsible advisers who did not have to answer to any legislative body for the counsel they gave to the President.

The growing strength of the Communists, mass unemployment, strikes, terrorism, and quasi-civil-war conditions made many think that Germany was headed for a Bolshevik revolution. The Communists seemed to have only one strong and uncompromising opponent: the Nazis. No longer did it seem to be a question of whether democratic or extremist forces were going to take control, but only whether the extremists in power would be the Nazis or the Communists. The sense of crisis was heightened in November 1932, when new Reichstag elections again did not produce a basis for a coalition government. Hindenburg dropped Papen and on 2 December appointed a new Chancellor, Armed Forces Minister Major General Kurt von Schleicher. The Reichstag had opposed Papen's government, and Schleicher had convinced Hindenburg that Papen's continuation in office would lead to a general strike, a civil war, and possibly a border war with Poland. Schleicher believed that he could find majority support in the Reichstag for a cabinet of his own. In this he failed, but his policy was otherwise promising. He worked patiently to achieve economic recovery and to curb the National Socialists, whose support had begun to decline.

The intriguers went to work on the President again. They included Papen; Otto Meissner, head of the presidential office; and Oskar von Hindenburg, the President's moderately capable but influential son, "for whom there was no provision in the Constitution," as a contemporary witticism had it.[8] Papen, hungering for power and revenge against Schleicher, told Hindenburg that he could produce a national coalition government, consisting of the German National People's Party, the National Socialists, and the veterans' organization "Der Stahlhelm." Schleicher, finding his position untenable vis-à-vis a hostile Reichstag and wanting to block the return of Papen, also supported Hitler's candidacy for Chancellor.

On 30 January 1933 Hindenburg appointed a new cabinet selected by Papen. It was headed by Hitler as Chancellor, with Papen as Vice Chancellor and temporary governor of Prussia, the largest state of Germany. The cabinet included only two Nazis besides Hitler—Wilhelm Frick as Minister of the Interior and Hermann Göring as Minister without Portfolio—but it had nine conservative ministers, including Alfred Hugenberg, the newspaper magnate and leader of the German National People's Party. The new Armed Forces minister in the cabinet, Field-marshal Werner von Blomberg, and his Undersecretary, General Walter von Reichenau, were supporters of Hitler. Frick controlled broad police powers. Göring was also Speaker of the Reichstag and Minister for Internal Affairs in Prussia. Hitler and his associates therefore controlled key positions. Soon they pushed aside Papen, Hugenberg, and other once powerful figures.

Popular support for the Nazis was always limited. At its highest it remained under 38 percent in free elections. Despite all the coercion and terrorism at the Nazis' command after five weeks in office, and despite massive threats and interference by Nazi organizations at polling stations, in elections on 5 March 1933 the Nazis still drew only 43.9 percent of the vote.[9] Considering the circumstances, this was a resounding rejection. There were no compelling constitutional or political reasons to make Hitler Chancellor. But there was good reason not to make him Chancellor: Hitler had made clear that he meant to destroy the Constitution, and thus his appointment as Chancellor violated the spirit of the Constitution. Popular support may have explained Hitler's political weight and his consideration for political office. But it was far from constituting majority support.

The role of "big business" in Hitler's rise to power was minimal, despite Marxist propaganda about the National Socialists as capitalist lackeys. Other than modest contributions from the occasional tycoon, big business did not support the Nazis generally, nor did it play a part in Hitler's appointment specifically.[10] Financial support from big business was negligible before 30 January 1933, and so was the role of a few minor businessmen. The meeting between Papen and Hitler on 4 January 1933 in Cologne to prepare a coalition cabinet took place in the house of a banker, Kurt von Schröder. Schröder himself had no influence in the matters discussed there, and anyone else of those few who were aware that Hitler and Papen were ready to reach an agreement could have performed the same service. What underlay the events was not some sinister impersonal force, and not class or business interests, but personal interests. Conspiracy and intrigue, not an overwhelming wave of national support, enabled a gang of political criminals to get hold of the state.

Consolidation of Power 2

The Nazis in the new cabinet moved immediately to exercise political power solely in the interests of their own party. Hitler began at once to turn his constitutional emergency government into a one-party dictatorship. The first step was to gain a favorable majority in the Reichstag, by hook or by crook. Hitler sought the President's approval for new elections, but the President insisted that Hitler negotiate to include another party, the Center Party, in his coalition in order to create a majority government. The Center Party was not unwilling to support the new government, under appropriate conditions, but Hitler did not really want any hindrances on his way to total power. He negotiated only for show. On 1 February 1933 the negotiations failed, as planned, and Hindenburg consented to new elections, to be held on March 5. The Center Party leader protested to Hindenburg that a coalition was still in the realm of possibility—and thus showed that he did not understand the forces with which he was dealing. Hindenburg could not reverse his decision without loss of authority.

On 3 February 1933, Reich Chancellor Hitler went to the Armed Forces Ministry on Bendlerstrasse and, in the private rooms of the Commander in Chief of the Army, addressed the senior Army and Navy commanders. He said that his overall policy was rearmament and the conquest of Lebensraum (territorial living space), which would involve defeating France first, for "if France has statesmen, she will not permit us to rearm." The generals were told not to worry about harsh measures that would be taken in internal matters, as these would be carried out by the Nazi organizations; the Armed Forces would not be involved.[1]

On the same day, Joseph Goebbels, Gauleiter (Nazi District Leader) for Berlin and the Chief of Propaganda in the NSDAP, wrote in his diary concerning the campaign for the Reichstag elections scheduled for 5 March: "The struggle is a light one now, since we are able to employ all means of the State. Radio and Press are at our disposal. We shall achieve a masterpiece of propaganda. Even money is not lacking this time . . . The Radio causes me some trouble. All the important positions are still held by the same old-System profiteers. They have to be got rid of as soon as possible, that is before the fifth of March, lest they endanger the election."[2] But the Nazis intended to go much farther.

On the following day, 4 February, at the National Socialists' request, Hindenburg signed the first of two emergency decrees which were presented as necessary for the internal security of Germany, but had the effect of turning over to the Nazis dictatorial powers.[3] This decree, titled Decree of the Reich President for the Protection of the German People, obliged organizers of political gatherings to register them with local police authorities at least forty-eight hours in advance, and it prohibited gatherings if "an immediate danger to public security was feared." The terms of the decree left the door open to arbitrary interpretation. It provided for an appeal, but one that could not suspend police action. Political rallies and open-air gatherings could be dissolved if the speakers encouraged disobedience to laws or to government authorities, "insulted or maliciously subjected to contempt" cabinet members or secretaries of state, or encouraged violent action against persons or objects. Police forces throughout Germany were authorized to send police officers to every political gathering and to insist that these officers be given a "suitable" place in the assembly. If they were not admitted on these terms, the gathering could be dissolved.

In addition, according to the decree, the Reich Minister of the Interior—the Nazi Frick—could prohibit "generally or conditionally for the entire Reich territory or parts thereof" open-air gatherings and the wearing of "uniform dress indicating membership in a political association." Regional state authorities could prohibit open-air gatherings only at specified localities and only in individual cases. If the Reich Minister of the Interior had "misgivings" regarding such a prohibition, he could request its repeal or could repeal it himself. Since most of the state governments were not yet under direct Nazi control, the Nazi Reich Minister was thus able to prevent restrictions on Nazi gatherings.

Similar stipulations in the decree applied to printed publications "whose content was apt to endanger public safety and order." Such publications could be confiscated by the police. The prohibition was directed against publications inciting to disobedience of laws, decrees, and ordinances; inciting to violent acts or glorification of violent acts, inciting to general strikes in "vital" establishments, vilifying religious associations, and making incorrect statements that might endanger the "vital interests of the state." Again, the Reich Minister of the Interior had authority to decide on appeals in the immediate term, although he was enjoined to seek a Reich Supreme Court decision if he could not settle an appeal satisfactorily by himself. For the immediate purposes of the electoral campaign, the Reich Minister was the ultimate authority.

All these measures may seem to have been merely bureaucratic or theoretical, but they were not. They enabled the Nazis to pervert justice and to exploit the government structure for their own purposes. Raids, confiscations of literature, arrests, acts of revenge, and street battles could all be legalized.

The range of powers transferred to the Nazis was extended by several additional measures. On 6 February 1933, Papen was appointed Reichskommissar (Governor) for the largest state of the Reich, Prussia.[4] But Göring was Prussia's Minister of the Interior, so that in Prussia a Nazi minister had direct control of the police.[5] Goebbels noted in his diary: "Goering is setting things to rights in Prussia with splendid energy. He is the sort of man who does a thing radically, and his nerves are made to

stand a hard fight."[6] Göring's authority did not extend to the
other German states, but Prussia was by far the largest and most
important.

Then on 17 February 1933, Göring, as Prussian Minister of
the Interior, issued a decree, under the title Advancement of the
National Movement, that the Prussian police must avoid so
much as an appearance of hostility toward "national organizations (SA [Sturmabteilung, or storm troopers], SS [Schutz-
staffel, or guard detachment] and Stahlhelm) and national parties,"
and that their activities must not be impeded by police restrictions except in the most urgent cases. By contrast, the activities
of organizations hostile to the state must be countered ruthlessly: "Communist terrorist acts and attacks must be met with
all severity and, when necessary, with ruthless use of the weapon.
I shall cover for police officers who use firearms in the discharge
of these duties regardless of the consequences of the use of
firearms. Those who display weakness, however, will be subject
to disciplinary action."[7] This was Göring's notorious Shooting
Ordinance.

On 22 February 1933, Göring issued a further ordinance for
Prussia, the Decree for the Recruitment and Deployment of
Auxiliary Police, to deputize "appropriate persons" as police
officers. Another order of the same day designated as auxiliary
police officers "for the time being only members of the SS, SA,
Stahlhelm, and the German-National Combat Group."[8] Fifty
thousand auxiliary officers were appointed in this way: 40,000
of these were SA and SS troopers. The thugs, vigilantes, hit
squads, and shock troops of the Nazi paramilitary organizations
now had free range. They set up illegal detention centers and
concentration camps. The camps were filled with Communists,
Social Democrats and other political opponents, writers suspected of "un-German" and "un-national" sentiments, students,
laborers, and criminals who were commonly used as assistants
to the camp masters. Beatings and killings became the order of
the day. If a death had to be acknowledged, the explanation
would be heart failure or the ominous words "shot while trying
to escape." Battles in the streets and in assembly halls were daily

events during the election campaign. Fifty-one people were killed, over and above those who died in camps and in police custody.

On 20 February 1933, Hitler addressed a small gathering of business and industry leaders in the President's Palace, saying: "We are facing the last election. However it turns out, there will never be a relapse, even if the election does not result in a decision. Regardless, if the election does not decide, the decision must be made through a different means. I have been in favor of giving the people once more the opportunity to decide their fate themselves."[9] Göring spoke after Hitler, saying that business and industry would have to contribute money to the Nazi and German National People's Party's election campaigns. Their financial burden surely would be lightened, he added, by the knowledge that the elections of 5 March would be the last ones for ten years and probably for a hundred years.

The Left was the principal target of the Nazi terror at the moment. The terror was one of the reasons that the Social Democrats, their paramilitary organizations, the trade unions, and the Communists did not organize and fight while they could. The Army was visibly on the Nazis' side. Another reason was that on the Left, as in other political quarters, many people underestimated the staying power of the Nazis, who were expected to fail like their predecessors. Finally, an economic depression, with mass unemployment, did not seem to the Social Democrats and trade unions to be an opportune time to call on those who were working to go out on a general strike. Many party and union officials, faced with the alternatives of concentration camp or emigration, left the country—temporarily, they believed. Many of those who stayed became prisoners in concentration camps or jails. The Communists for their part fought the Social Democrats as bitterly as they fought the Nazis, for the preservation of the Bolshevik Revolution in Josef Stalin's view required a balance of power among the capitalist states, whereas the Social Democrats advocated a reconciliation between France and Germany. The KPD followed the Moscow line.[10]

In this situation, the burning of the Reichstag building on 27

February 1933 was a windfall for the Nazis.[11] The weight of the evidence supports the finding by the Reich Supreme Court that a Dutch anarchist with some Communist background had set the fire. It was therefore easy to blame "the Communists." This could be used to expand the government's emergency powers. But the Communist Party was not outlawed—perhaps because it would have required complicated procedures to outlaw a political party, but certainly because large numbers of Communist voters might have then supported the Social Democrats, threatening the projected Nazi voting majority. The better tactic was to deprive the elected Communists of their seats later.

A new and hastily drafted presidential emergency decree, titled Decree of the Reich President for the Protection of the People and the State, received the President's signature on 28 February 1933, the day after the fire.[12] "In defense against Communist state-endangering violent acts," the decree provided for a sweeping suspension of the articles in the Constitution guaranteeing personal liberty, freedom of speech and the press, freedom of assembly and association, freedom of communication (mails, telegraphs, telephones), protection against search and seizure in the home, and freedom of property. The police could arrest persons without a warrant and without stating any reasons; they could hold persons indefinitely, search their homes, and confiscate their property. In states where "the measures necessary to restore public security and order" were not taken, the Reich government could assume executive power. Some crimes that had carried a life sentence henceforth carried a mandatory death penalty, including attempts and conspiracies to kill the President or a commissar of the government, treason against the government, poisoning of individuals, willful flooding, damage to railway installations, and poisoning dangerous to the public. The attempt to commit a crime in each case carried the same penalty as the accomplished deed.

There had been emergency decrees before. But they had been issued when it was a question of enacting essential legislation, such as budgets or relief measures. Now the emergency decrees, though described as necessary to save the state from threats to its security, served only to consolidate and expand the National Socialists' power and the government's independence of parliamentary control.

The presidential emergency decree of 28 February 1933, soon called the Reichstag Fire Decree, was based on unproven assumptions. The arsonist was tried in the Reich Supreme Court, which concluded that there had not been a Communist conspiracy, thus voiding the basis of the decree. But the decree was not repealed before the end of the Second World War, and throughout its twelve years in effect, it was used extensively, notably against the churches and against the Resistance. The government had suspended fundamental constitutional rights on the basis of unproven, later disproven, assumptions. It acted illegally, even within its own dubious standards, throughout its tenure.

Democracy had first been abolished through presidential decree. The Constitution gave the President emergency powers, and he had been led to use them to destroy the Constitution itself. With the makeshift decree of 28 February, the Nazi government wiped out every protection of human freedom that had been achieved through the centuries in the West. In establishing lawlessness and arbitrary rule as the "legal" basis of the Nazi state, the Reichstag Fire Decree became the constitution of the state.[13] It legalized a permanent state of siege.

The atmosphere in which the elections were held on 5 March 1933 was dominated by terror. There were beatings, shootings, arbitrary arrests, vast propaganda activities, and mass marches of Nazi troopers, creating a state close to civil war. Thousands of Center and Left party functionaries were arrested. The Communist press was banned, as was the Social Democrat press temporarily. In thousands of polling stations uniformed SA or SS men looked over peoples' shoulders as they marked their ballots.

The elections gave the NSDAP 43.9 percent of the popular vote, well short of the absolute majority they had wanted.[14] They gained 288 seats out of a total of 647. The government controlled a majority of seats through a coalition with the 52 seats held by the German National People's Party. The Communist Party received 4.8 million votes, or 12.3 percent of the vote; the Social Democrats received 18.3 percent of the vote; the Center Party received 11.2 percent; and smaller parties got the rest. The majority of the voters did *not* endorse Hitler's government and denied him their support.

The mandate of voters in that "last," no more than partially free election of 5 March 1933 was less than satisfactory from the Nazis' point of view. Further measures were needed to give Hitler's government a secure tenure. Numerous other emergency decrees appeared. Twenty such decrees were issued in the first two months after Hitler's appointment as Chancellor. Three of these decrees were particularly pernicious.

The first one, dated 28 February 1933, was titled Decree of the Reich President against Treason toward the German People and against High Treasonous Machinations. It imposed a penalty of imprisonment for the communication to foreign governments of statements of fact.[15] It did not matter whether the facts reported were true or false. It also did not matter whether they were in the public domain or were already known to the foreign governments in question.

The second decree, dated 21 March 1933, was titled Decree of the Reich President for Defense against Insidious Attacks against the Government of the National Resurgence. It declared that saying anything factually untrue was a punishable crime, if the statement was potentially damaging to state interests or to government prestige. It made criticism of the government and of its officials a crime. If the "deed" was committed with the intention of causing unrest among the population or creating difficulty for the German Reich abroad, "terms in penitentiary of not less than three years, or life, must be imposed. In particularly serious cases the death penalty may be imposed."[16] Thus a mere decree, not a law, declared certain acts to be punishable crimes. Furthermore, this was not a decree against treason or the disclosure of state secrets, because a law of long standing already protected state secrets whose revelation could be detrimental to the defense and integrity of the nation.

The third of these extraordinary decrees, the Decree of the Reich Government for the Constitution of Special Courts, also issued on 21 March 1933, was the logical complement of the Insidiousness Decree.[17] It set up special courts (Sondergerichte) in every superior-court district. These courts were given jurisdiction in all cases arising out of both the Reichstag Fire Decree and the Insidiousness Decree. All decisions on pretrial detention of the accused were placed in the hands of the special court's presiding judge; there was no hearing; appeals were judged by the same special court against whose decisions they had been brought. The special courts were given authority to arrest and detain any suspect, anywhere, for any length of time. They were also given the quasi-legal authority to maintain concentration camps. The special courts could judge cases without hearing evidence. The special court, according to the decree, "must pass judgment and sentence even in cases which turn out not to be within its jurisdiction," unless the cases were within the jurisdiction of the Reich Supreme Court or a state court of appeal. The special courts could hear cases that were under the jurisdiction of an ordinary court of law. Appeals against judgments of a special court were inadmissible.

An enabling act was proposed for passage by the Reichstag to cement Nazi power in more permanent legal terms than did the decrees. The act was intended to alter the Constitution "legally" and give permanence to the suspension of both individual liberties and constitutional checks and balances. President von Hindenburg was not always predictable, as he had demonstrated by dropping three Chancellors—Brüning, Papen, and Schleicher—in less than a year. He might be persuaded to suspend the emergency decrees as well. The enabling act was meant to secure dictatorial powers for Hitler for four years. The proposed act required two-thirds of the Reichstag votes for passage, but the coalition of the Nazi and German National People's parties fell short of a two-thirds majority. Other parties were needed to support the bill.

As a step in this direction, the Nazis had arrested many of the 81 Communist Reichstag deputies before the election. After the election, the Speaker, Göring, excluded all Communist deputies from attendance.[18] Hitler's policy was to consolidate an anti-Left front of all "national" Germans, for he dared not provoke the political competition in the Center and on the Right by dealing with them as he had with Communists and Social Democrats. He lured the Center Party into voting for the enabling act with a promise not to abuse the powers of the act. In the end, all parties voted for the act except the Communists, who were excluded, and the Social Democrats, who lost a gallant fight in the Reichstag. The vote on 23 March 1933 was 444 to 94 in favor of the act.[19]

The enabling act, titled Law to Remedy the Distress of the People and Reich, made it "constitutional" for the cabinet to pass laws without Reichstag approval. Legislative powers were now merged with the powers of the executive.[20] Furthermore, the cabinet could issue laws setting aside any part of the Constitution, and treaties with foreign states no longer required Reichstag ratification. The law was to remain in force only until April 1937, but it was renewed for another four years in 1937, rubber-stamped by the Nazi-controlled Reichstag, and it was renewed again in 1939. In 1943 Hitler decreed another extension by a Führer Ordinance, a personal order he issued without bothering to involve the Reichstag.[21] The government had then no legal existence, even according to its own standards of legality.

In addition to vastly expanding police and judicial powers, Hitler's government perfected political and administrative control at every level. The Reichstag Fire Decree had laid the basis for tightening government control; the enabling act continued the process and "simplified legislation." The Preliminary Law for the Co-ordination of the States and the Reich, issued on 31 March 1933, gave control over state governments to the central Reich authority.[22] State legislative assemblies and cabinets were reconstituted with proportionate party representation as it obtained at the level of the Reich. Nazi state governors were appointed by the central government.

After passage of the enabling act in the Reichstag on 23 March 1933, the old political parties disappeared one by one. The Communist Party had already lost its elected deputies through arrests between 5 and 21 March 1933. This kind of arrest was called "protective custody"; the government considered the method as not in conflict with concepts of parliamentary immunity.[23] The Social Democratic Party was formally outlawed on 22 June 1933 for "treasonous activities."[24] The German National People's Party dissolved itself on 27 June. The rest of the parties except for the Communists did the same, the last being the Center Party on 5 July. The Communist Party did not dissolve itself, nor was it formally outlawed, but like all other parties, on 14 July 1933 it lost its basis of existence through a piece of legislation called the Law Prohibiting the New Formation of Parties.[25]

Declaring the revolution completed, Hitler held a plebiscite in November 1933, in which 96.3 percent of all eligible voters cast ballots, and 95 percent of those who voted approved of the government's internal and external policies. There was only one party, no alternatives; but the figures themselves indicate that they were obtained through coercion and fraud. In December Hitler issued a law declaring the "unity of party and state."[26] It meant that the Nazi Party machine had taken over the German state and nation. All key positions in government and civil service were to be held by Nazi Party members. The law also meant that after the political revolution, there would not follow much of the economic and social revolution so eagerly anticipated by radicals in the party, including hundreds of thousands of SA storm troopers.

This law gave fair warning to Ernst Röhm, leader of the SA, who had always planned to make his organization the leading military establishment and to put it in control of the economy as well as of foreign and internal policies.[27] By the beginning of 1934 the SA ranks had swollen to over three million members. If the SA could cause chaos by starting a "social revolution" through expropriations of businesses and industries as well as through mass enlistments in the Army, Hitler's position would become dependent on the good will of the SA—which is to say, Röhm would become the real dictator of Germany.

There was already talk in the SA that Hitler had "betrayed the revolution." Röhm and his friends in the SA leadership corps wanted to merge the SA with the Army to form a National Socialist, and truly socialist, people's army, and they wanted to eliminate the professional officer corps. The Army in fact needed suitable recruits for a cautious expansion of its ranks, but certainly not the hundreds of thousands of SA storm troopers. Such numbers could not be absorbed and trained properly with the available experienced staff. Moreover, most of the storm troopers were not suitable because of their advanced age, and most of them were too undisciplined and difficult to integrate into the small, highly trained, professional Army. This professional Army would have been taken over, in effect, by inductions of storm troopers on the scale Röhm proposed.[28] Hitler himself considered the SA unusable militarily and dangerous internally.[29] Finally, if Germany expanded her armed forces too rapidly and too obviously, certain signatories of the Treaty of Versailles might decide to enforce its military restrictions. Hitler's government would then be doomed. Before expansion of the armed forces and rearmament, such a challenge could not be met.

Hitler had come to value the forms of legality and stability. His failure in the 1923 putsch, partly through lack of Army support, had been a traumatic lesson. He knew that he must never again lose the Army's support and loyalty. Moreover, an open eruption of the rivalry between the SA and the Reichswehr could seriously erode his authority. The Army, under the leadership of the Armed Forces Minister, Fieldmarshal von Blomberg, cooperated with Hitler.

A courageous speech by Vice Chancellor von Papen at the University of Marburg on 17 June 1934 helped to bring matters to a head. Papen spoke against suppression of freedom of speech, "unnatural totalitarianism," the one-party system, political invasions in the sphere of religion, contempt for the human spirit, and an "odious personality cult." With reference to the SA-Reichswehr rivalry, he challenged Hitler to accept his responsibility and act. Hitler was duly alarmed about the apparent cooperation between the Reichswehr and conservative circles around Papen, the ambitious former Chancellor.

The Reichswehr leaders were persuaded by Hitler and Göring of the dangers posed by obscure and sinister plans of the SA. Lists of potentially troublesome persons were prepared in the offices of Göring, Heinrich Himmler, and Reinhard Heydrich, Himmler's deputy, either in consultation with Hitler or in some cases independently.[30] These lists included such figures as former Chancellors Schleicher and probably Papen, the prominent Catholic leader Erich Klausener, and Hitler's old rival Gregor Strasser, the former Gauleiter of Lower Bavaria and Nazi Propaganda Leader. Papen was ultimately spared, most probably because Hitler feared that if Papen were shot, Hindenburg might intervene. Papen offered his resignation from his cabinet post on 3 July and accepted an appointment as diplomatic envoy to Austria on 26 July.[31]

At dawn on 30 June 1934, Hitler motored to Bad Wiessee, south of Munich, where Röhm and many of his friends were vacationing and where Hitler had suddenly scheduled a leadership conference. Accompanied by bodyguards, Hitler went into Röhm's hotel, ordered him out of bed, and had him and his staff arrested. They were taken to a Munich prison, where all except Röhm were shot within hours. Röhm himself was shot on 1 July, having refused to commit suicide. Dozens of other SA leaders were intercepted on the roads leading to Bad Wiessee, on trains arriving in Munich, and elsewhere in Germany. Hitler admitted in the Reichstag on 13 July that 74 persons had been shot and declared the executions emergency defensive measures; he called three of the deaths suicides. The final toll of deaths was 85.

On 3 July 1934, Hitler issued a law, countersigned by the Justice Minister, declaring the shootings "lawful."[32] The Reichswehr Minister, the Commander in Chief of the Army, and the Chief of the General Staff of the Army (then still called Chief

of Troops Office), did not protest openly against the murder by
Nazi thugs of two general officers, Schleicher and his assistant,
Ferdinand von Bredow. When General von Witzleben, Com-
manding General of the Third Army Corps and Military District
III (Berlin), asked for a court-martial hearing on the matter, the
Commander in Chief of the Army, General Werner Freiherr von
Fritsch, replied that he had heard from Blomberg that Hitler
had proof of Schleicher's treason.[33] Several other demands for
court-martial hearings were equally ineffective.

Hitler's next coup in consolidating his power was coupled
with President von Hindenburg's approaching death. The President had been ailing, and his death was clearly imminent. On
1 August 1934 Hitler issued the Law about the Head of State
of the German Reich, which declared the posts of Chancellor
and President combined. The words of the law specifically limited its application to one person: "1. The post of Reich President will be combined with that of the Reich Chancellor.
Therefore the powers of the Reich President devolve upon the
Reich Chancellor Adolf Hitler. He will determine his deputy.
2. This law becomes effective at the time of the death of Reich
President von Hindenburg."[34]

Hindenburg died the next day, on 2 August 1934. On the
same day, Reichswehr Minister von Blomberg administered a
new oath to the Armed Forces, in which all soldiers swore
personal, "unconditional obedience" to Adolf Hitler—not to
the nation, the Constitution, or even the people, just to Adolf
Hitler.[35] The Reichswehr leaders had become accomplices in
Hitler's murders. They had acquiesced in the murder of the SA
leaders and of two members of their own ranks, and they now
sealed their moral corruption with a personal oath to the chief
criminal who had boasted of his crimes in public. To Hitler, it
must have been clear that he had little to fear anymore from
that quarter.

Hitler had gone to the brink, as he had many times in his
career, and he had won. He came away from the SA crisis with
blood on his hands, as everyone could see, but also with the

reputation of one who knows when to strike hard. The population was more in awe of him than ever; popular confidence was enhanced in mysterious, atavistic ways. Hitler's confidence in his own ability to survive, to lead, to concentrate power in his hands, and to get his way was strengthened vastly. The next step was to end Germany's isolation in foreign policy.

Toward World Conquest   3

The Gestapo terrorized dissidents with the mere possibility of a knock on the door at five o'clock in the morning and two leather-coated figures standing outside saying, "Come with us." Gestapo cellars and concentration camps, torture and murder, completed the vision. Everyone had to expect to have his telephone tapped; people who feared that conversations in a room could be listened in to put pillows and blankets over their telephones. The Gestapo watched constantly for signs of opposition, breaking up Communist cells, confiscating pamphlets that had been smuggled into Germany by Social Democrat leaders in exile in Prague, and harassing Catholic priests or monks and Protestant ministers with charges of deviant behavior, subversion, and currency violations—the last a method serving also to curtail contacts with the Vatican or with the World Council of Churches in Geneva.

Freedom of the press disappeared. Other liberties were restricted, such as freedom to choose a workplace or a place of residence. Travel abroad was complicated by bureaucratic procedures and foreign-currency restrictions. Listening to foreign radio broadcasts was forbidden. During the war, people were sentenced to death and beheaded for doing so.

At the same time, work projects went forward. Road construction went forward on a vast scale. Dikes and factory buildings went up. A Nazi Party meeting arena was built in Nürnberg, and a new art museum and party administration buildings in Munich. Albert Speer was appointed Inspector General for building projects in the national capital, and Hitler set about reshaping Berlin. Superhighway construction, compulsory labor service, the introduction in March 1935 of general military conscription, the launching of a Four-Year Plan in August 1936 to raise Germany out of depression to economic self-sufficiency, and the armaments industry—all were major factors in producing full employment by 1938.[1] By 1939, however, these methods led Germany to the brink of financial ruin.[2] Göring, who was in charge of carrying out the Four-Year Plan, had proclaimed as its motto "Guns instead of butter"; in fact, butter had to be rationed even before the war. Territorial acquisitions later obscured an astronomical debt and the devaluation of the currency.

In foreign affairs, Hitler had moved cautiously in the first years of his reign. He had taken as his foreign minister an experienced and respected civil servant, Constantin Baron von Neurath. Nevertheless, Germany became increasingly isolated in the first half of 1933. Hitler's rise to power was viewed with suspicion in foreign capitals, as the German government observed the military stipulations of the Treaty of Versailles less and less by demanding equal rights and pursuing more vigorously a policy of limited rearmament that had been begun before 1933. The anti-Jewish "boycott" of 1 April 1933, involving terror activities against Jews and Jewish businesses, had not helped Germany's reputation abroad; indeed, the reaction abroad was so negative and the threat to Germany's foreign trade so serious that the boycott activities were stopped at once.

But on 20 July 1933, Hitler achieved an agreement with far-reaching implications. He concluded a concordat with the Vatican which regulated the status of Catholic institutions in Germany and the freedom of Catholics to worship.[3] There had not been a concordat with a German central government since the Reformation. The new concordat was signed by Cardinal State Secretary Eugenio Pacelli (later Pope Pius XII) and Vice Chancellor Franz von Papen. Since the Catholic Church in Germany was less closely linked with the government than were the Protestant churches (Lutheran and Reformed), this agreement was valuable from the Catholic point of view because it gave the church a firmer, more defensible legal position. For Hitler, however, the concordat was a signal to the entire world that his government was respectable and trustworthy in the eyes of the highest authority of Catholicism. It also gave Hitler leverage for rallying to his government the support of the German Catholics, as he commented in a telegram to Papen which was published in the official Nazi Party newspaper, the *Völkischer Beobachter*. The dissolution of the Center Party, the organization of political Catholicism in Germany, thus appeared to be sanctioned by the church.

At the urging of Mussolini, Hitler had agreed on 15 July 1933 to join in a Four-Power Pact with France, Britain, and Italy which aimed in general terms at concerted policies, but he did not really care for collective agreements.[4] When in October 1933 the British Foreign Secretary, Sir John Simon, proposed to the Geneva Disarmament Conference, at which Germany was represented, a plan to postpone Germany's equality in armaments for four years, Hitler took the occasion to withdraw the German delegation from the conference and to resign membership in the League of Nations.[5] Hitler had concludeed that Germany could make more rapid progress in rearming and in regaining its proper status as a Great Power if it moved independently of collective commitments and used instead the method of bilateral agreement.

His next foreign policy maneuver was nothing less than a coup. Poland had apparently negotiated with France to bring about some preventive action, possibly a reoccupation of certain German territories, with the purpose of holding Hitler to the Treaty of Versailles, but France had declined. The Polish government resorted to the alternative of seeking an agreement with Germany. For Hitler, it was important to keep potential enemies from combining against Germany during the phase of rearmament that exposed it to foreign intervention and to internal tensions. Consequently, Germany signed the German-Polish Nonaggression Treaty on 26 January 1934. It stunned the diplomatic world, demonstrating that Germany could not be kept in isolation. A serious breach had been achieved in France's elaborate system of alliances among states bordering on Germany.

France and the Soviet Union understood this outcome. On 2 May 1935 they concluded an anti-German mutual defense pact.[6] This was a setback for Hitler, but there were other fronts on which he was successful.

On 13 January 1935 the population of the Saar Region, which had been under French administration since the First World War, voted overwhelmingly to return to Germany, in a plebiscite that had been stipulated by the Treaty of Versailles.[7] The people of the Saar preferred a national dictatorship to semiautonomy under a foreign authority. Their decision was a defeat for democracy and a victory for nationalism.[8]

Hitler's next move, undertaken on the pretext that all efforts to bring about multilateral disarmament had come to naught, was to proclaim universal military service in Germany on 16 March 1935. There were protests, but only protests. Sir John Simon and Anthony Eden were due to visit the German capital on 25 March. Instead of canceling, the British government asked, in the concluding paragraph of its protest note, whether the German government still wished to proceed with the state visit.[9] The visit took place as planned. At a conference in Stresa in April, Britain, France, and Italy condemned Hitler's move. But on 18 June 1935, Hitler concluded a naval agreement with Britain in which Britain agreed to a German fleet at 35 percent of the strength of the British fleet, with parity in submarines. The British Admiralty was concerned to prevent a naval armaments race similar to that before the First World War, and it considered Japan a looming menace. But the German-British agreement undermined the objections to Hitler's violations of the Treaty of Versailles—violations that Britain, France, and Italy had just condemned.[10] Hitler could hardly help concluding that the brutal method was the correct one in foreign policy as well as in domestic affairs.

Less than a year later, on 7 March 1936, Hitler ordered troops into the Rhineland. Although this was German territory, the

Treaty of Versailles prohibited the presence of German troops there. The few German units that crossed the line into the demilitarized zone were greeted by enthusiastic applause from the population.[11] Again, verbal protests were the only consequence.

The Olympic Summer Games were held in Berlin in 1936 with pomp and organizational skill. A string of French and British government ministers and other dignitaries passed through Hitler's Chancellery in Berlin and his vacation retreat near Berchtesgaden. In the autumn of 1937, the Duke of Windsor and Lord Halifax came to see Hitler.[12] There seemed to be no end of recognition, and no end of success.

A fortnight before Hitler received Lord Halifax at his Berchtesgaden retreat, the "Berghof," he had addressed the War Minister, Field Marshal von Blomberg, the Foreign Minister, Baron von Neurath, and the heads of the military services in the Reich Chancellery in Berlin, on 5 November 1937: Commander in Chief of the Army, General Baron von Fritsch, Commander in Chief of the Navy, Admiral Erich Raeder, and Commander in Chief of the Air Force, General Göring. Hitler's Wehrmacht Adjutant, Colonel Friedrich Hossbach, who was also present, recorded what was said in the meeting.[13] Hitler said that the German people needed more space and the Armed Forces, equipped with modern equipment, were nearly ready to move, but that the Nazi Party was aging and by 1943–1945 the military equipment would have become obsolete. Therefore it was necessary to "act" (read: "go to war") before this happened. Germany might "act" even earlier if France became so beset by internal difficulties that it could not intervene. Hitler claimed that "almost certainly Britain, and probably France as well, had already tacitly written off the Czechs," and so the opportunity "must be seized upon whenever it occurs for the blow against the Czechs." If France, Italy, and England were involved in a Mediterranean war, Germany would have to attack Czechoslovakia and Austria simultaneously. Both of these moves were only preparatory to "the improvement of our politico-military position . . . in order to remove the threat to our flank in any possible operation against the West." Hitler did not state in detail that he intended to conquer "living space" in the East on a large scale, but the nexus is unmistakable between the immediately possible "actions" against Czechoslovakia, Austria, and "the West" and his "unalterable resolve to solve Germany's problem of space at the latest by 1943–45." If Britain and France had written off Czechoslovakia, they were not presumed to have written off Poland, Rumania, Bulgaria, Hungary, and Russia as well.

Blomberg and Fritsch insisted that Britain and France must not be put in the position of enemies of Germany, that the French forces were superior to the German forces, and that the German western fortifications were insignificant, whereas the Czech fortifications were formidable. Neurath objected that a favorable situation—an Anglo-French-Italian conflict—was not likely within the foreseeable future. Hitler countered that the opportunity would probably occur in the summer of 1938. Raeder was not recorded as objecting, but even Göring objected, though cautiously, by saying that under the circumstances the German intervention in the Spanish Civil War on the side of Franco's forces would have to be ended. The meeting then turned to the details of armaments, and this may have enabled Hitler to save face. The bare fact was that he had received some strong objections to his views and no support at all from anyone present at the meeting.

This was an extraordinary situation. The chiefs of the Armed Forces had said no to the directives of their Supreme Commander and Head of State. Hitler had to conclude that he would have nothing but trouble from this crew. As Field Marshal Erich von Manstein put it after the war at the Nürnberg trial: "Under a dictatorship, a dictator cannot permit himself to be forced, because the moment he gives way, his dictatorship ends."[14] Within three months of Hitler's meeting with the Armed Forces leaders, only Raeder and Göring still held their positions. Blomberg had plunged headlong into a scandal, apparently with a good deal of help from Göring, by marrying a woman with an unacceptable past. He was forced to resign.[15] At the same time Gestapo officers reconstituted a file that Hitler had ordered destroyed in 1936, containing the allegation by a convicted blackmailer that Fritsch had been involved in homosexual activities. Fritsch, too, was driven to resignation. Although a High Court Martial later exposed the accuser as a pathological liar and Fritsch was rehabilitated, Hitler had had his way, and the damage was done. The appointment of General Walther von Brauchitsch as Fritsch's successor was made possible when Hitler offered him substantial financial aid to resolve an untidy divorce affair. Hitler did not mind applying a double standard. The gift also obligated Brauchitsch to Hitler, and Brauchitsch was in any case willing to do Hitler's bidding.

Hitler had brought off a new coup d'état similar to the usurpation of the Presidency and the imposition of the personal oath in August 1934. He did not appoint a new War Minister but assumed direct personal command of the Wehrmacht and of the functions of the War Minister. Henceforth Hitler controlled the War Ministry through an office chief, General Wilhelm Keitel, who was called Chief of the Wehrmacht Supreme Command (OKW).[16] Neurath was replaced by the German Ambassador in London, Joachim von Ribbentrop. A number of other military and diplomatic functionaries who were known to be reluctant to support Hitler on his adventurous course were replaced as well.

Hitler had once again treated the Army with abuse and insult. When in 1934 two general officers had been shot by Nazi thugs, nothing had happened. Now in 1938 a Field Marshal had been encouraged to involve himself in scandal, and the Commander in Chief of the Army had been framed deliberately. Again, as in 1934, it was not easy for those distant from events in Berlin to see to the bottom of the affair. Again, however, attitudes among the senior officer corps helped Hitler to bring off his coup.

Riding a wave of success and confidence, Hitler bullied the Austrian Chancellor Kurt von Schuschnigg on 12 February 1938 at his Berghof vacation house and forced him into accepting an Austrian Nazi, Artur Seyss-Inquart, as Minister of the Interior and Minister for Security. This agent of Hitler's thought that a military occupation of Austria was unnecessary for unification with Germany. When told by Göring to send a telegram requesting military assistance, Seyss-Inquart balked. After Schuschnigg on 9 March announced a plebiscite on Austria's independence, Hitler on 10 March ordered the invasion of Austria, which succeeded triumphantly on 12 March.[17] The population cheered the German troops.

A few weeks later in March 1938 Hitler ordered the Army to be ready for the invasion of Czechoslovakia. As a pretext for his intended invasion, he demanded the unification with Germany of the German-speaking Sudetenland, a part of Czechoslovakia. This demand led to the notorious Munich Agreement of 29 September, reached at a conference attended by Germany, Italy, Britain, and France, at which the four countries agreed to amputate Czechoslovakia. Hitler had wanted to occupy all of Czechoslovakia, but he was deterred by Mussolini's refusal to back him and by Britain's and France's military preparations.[18] He signed an international multilateral treaty that gave him the German-speaking Sudeten region.

Anti-Jewish policies had been in effect in Germany since the beginning of Nazi rule. A nationwide "boycott" of Jews was declared on 1 April 1933. This involved blacklisting, looting and destroying Jewish businesses, pillorying Jews, and verbally and physically attacking Jewish physicians and lawyers in particular. The boycott lasted only twenty-four hours, mainly because of adverse publicity abroad which threatened Germany's foreign trade. The clamor of anti-Jewish campaigns was muffled afterward, but the policies continued. Dozens of discriminatory laws and ordinances were issued against Jews in the civil service, in the universities, in the arts, in science, in the legal and medical professions, in journalism and literature, and against converted Jews in the churches. In 1935 the so-called Nürnberg racial laws were promulgated to define Jews. These laws used the criteria of religion, ancestry, and German citizenship. Marriage between Jews and non-Jews was prohibited, and extramarital sexual contact between Jews and non-Jews was subject to criminal prosecution.

In August 1936 Hitler wrote a secret memorandum for a Four-Year Plan. In September 1936 its concepts, aimed at preparing Germany economically for war, were published. But the secret memorandum coupled measures against the Jews and their "punishment" with the concerns of a war economy by demanding two new laws: one "providing the death penalty for economic sabotage," and the other "making the whole of Jewry liable for all damage inflicted by individual specimens of this community of criminals upon the German economy, and thus upon the German people."[19] There was a deep coherence in this connection. The war against the Jews was linked with and covered up by an ordinary war of imperial conquest. Hitler's obsession with destroying the Jews broke through the seemingly rational, organized surface of life in the Nazi state again and again. In a speech before the Gauleiters in April 1937, Hitler remarked in the context of refusing, for the moment, to increase the tempo and severity of measures against the Jews: "The final aim of our whole policy is perfectly clear to all of us."[20]

In 1938 new restrictions were placed on Jews, to eliminate them from the German economy and to reduce their numbers through emigration.[21] One ordinance required all Jews to report their assets. Both the internal revenue service and the local police were provided with lists of wealthy Jews. There were waves of arrests, primarily of Jews who had criminal records and Jews who were regarded as shirkers and vagrants.

Matters came to a head with the issuance by the Polish government of new directives for all Polish passport holders in Germany. In July 1933 the Nazi government had deprived of German citizenship all Jews who had immigrated since 1918 from territories that had become Polish after the First World War. In response, the Polish embassy in Berlin had issued Polish passports to many but not all of these Jews. In the autumn of 1938 the Polish authorities feared that, if the German authorities expelled the Jews with Polish passports, Poland would have to admit them. The Polish government sought to block such an eventuality by ordering, on short notice, a review of all Polish passport holders in Germany and by declaring invalid the passports of Polish citizens who had lived abroad for five years. The German government did not wait for the review but arrested over 15,000 of these persons on 27 and 28 October and tried to deport them to Poland. For a time the Polish authorities refused to admit them, so that they wandered helplessly in the no man's land, trying to cross the border.

When Herschel Grynzpan, the son of one of the deportees, in revenge shot Ernst vom Rath, a German embassy official in Paris, Hitler either initiated or tolerated an anti-Jewish pogrom which began on the night of 9 November 1938 and continued to 11 November. Under orders of their superior officers, SA men burned and vandalized Jewish synagogues and smashed Jewish shops. A circular of 9 November to all Gestapo offices ordered the police "not to disturb the actions against synagogues," to secure important archival material, and to make arrangements to prevent "looting and other excesses." It ordered preparations for the arrest of twenty to thirty thousand wealthy Jews and it ordered the "severest measures" against Jews found in possession of weapons. A high-ranking SA leader reported in subsequent Nazi Party investigations into deaths of Jews during the pogrom that he had been ordered to "disarm all Jews, and to shoot them down if they resisted." He was also to post signs on all Jewish shops, synagogues, "etc.," reading "Revenge for the murder of vom Rath, death to international Jewry, no understanding with people who are influenced by Jews." Ninety-one Jews were murdered; twenty-six thousand were arrested and taken to concentration camps in Dachau, Buchenwald, and Sachsenhausen. Finally, the German Jewish community was ordered to pay one billion marks in "restitution."

This pogrom indicated what was to come. The robbing of Jews and their elimination from German life had been proceeding since 1933. Murder had also been an instrument of Nazi rule from its first day. Now the murder of Jews was encouraged if in the judgment of SA leaders the circumstances justified the "severest measures." Everyone understood that murder was murder and that no law or ordinance could change that. Therefore the murder of Jews could not be ordered openly; it could only be ordered under cover terms, such as "severest measures" or, later, "special treatment" and "final solution."[22]

Again the concepts of war and of the destruction of Jews were proceeding in striking juxtaposition in Hitler's mind. He regarded the two ideas as synonymous throughout his career. In a speech on 10 November 1938 to German journalists and publishers in Munich while the pogrom was raging throughout Germany—while "they burned all the meeting places of God in the land" (Psalm 74)—Hitler spoke exclusively of war. In a speech on 30 January 1939, as he prepared Germany for war, he threatened the total destruction of European Jewry. And when in October 1939 he gave a formal order to kill the mentally ill and the feeble, which laid the technical foundations for the Holocaust of the Jews, he had the order back-dated to 1 September 1939, the day he had begun the war against Poland.[23]

During the Sudeten crisis Hitler found that the German people had a negative attitude toward war. They failed to cheer on 27 September 1938 when the Second Motorized Division from Stettin was marched through the streets of Berlin as a demonstration of strength.[24] According to a Nazi report, the people were "serious and silent" as they observed the division moving past the Reich Chancellery in Berlin. William Shirer, a correspondent for the American Columbia Broadcasting System in Berlin, wrote in his diary about the same event:

> A motorized division rolled through the city's streets just at dusk this evening in the direction of the Czech frontier. I went out to the corner of the Linden where the column was turning down the Wilhelmstrasse, expecting to see a tremendous demonstration. I pictured the scenes I had read of in 1914 when the cheering throngs on this same street tossed flowers at the marching soldiers, and the girls ran up and kissed them. The hour was undoubtedly chosen today to catch the hundreds of thousands of Berliners pouring out of their offices at the end of the day's work. But they ducked into the subways, refused to look on, and the handful that did stood at the curb in utter silence unable to find a word of cheer for the flower of their youth going away to the glorious war. It has been the most striking demonstration against the war I've ever seen. Hitler himself reported furious. I had not been

standing long at the corner when a policeman came up the Wilhelmstrasse from the direction of the Chancellery and shouted to the few of us standing at the curb that the Führer was on his balcony reviewing the troops. Few moved. I went down to have a look. Hitler stood there, and there weren't two hundred people in the street or the great square of the Wilhelmsplatz. Hitler looked grim, then angry, and soon went inside, leaving his troops to parade by unreviewed. What I've seen tonight almost rekindles a little faith in the German people. They are dead set against war.[25]

This background explains Hitler's speech to the press on 10 November 1938.[26] The task of propaganda, said Hitler, was to prepare the German people slowly. "Circumstances have forced me for decades to speak almost exclusively of peace." Peace propaganda had been the only way of bringing about the necessary rearmament, but it had its questionable aspects, in that it could mislead people about the true aims of the government. The German people must now be made to understand that certain things could be achieved only through force. The correct method was not to preach force, but to show the people certain foreign policy matters in such a light that they themselves would gradually demand the use of force. The other powers had become aware of Germany's policies and were making ready to oppose them, so that now was the last possible moment to solve the problem of Czechoslovakia. Preparations, according to Hitler, "for the first time had to be made with a view to the ultimate consequence, and they were so enormous that camouflage no longer seemed conceivable . . . under these circumstances the world would not have been deceived by it. Somehow I believe that this record, the pacifist record, has played itself out here . . . I was convinced that there was now only the other method, namely, to state the truth ruthlessly, no more and no less . . . In the end, success decides."

The people had come through when necessary, and the power of the press to ensure this was enormous. Hitler had only one worry: "When I look at our intellectuals, regrettably, one needs them; otherwise one could one day, well, I do not know, exterminate them or something." But the entire people "must learn to believe so fanatically in the final victory that any defeats we might suffer would be viewed only from the superior consideration that this was temporary. In the end, victory will be ours . . . It is certain that one decision must be taken now . . . It is therefore of no consequence whatsoever whether such a decision is entirely correct in the end; this is entirely without interest. What is decisive is that such a decision is backed up by the entire nation as by troops with closed ranks." This statement was a tidy summary of Hitler's compulsion to limitless gambles and of his demonic indifference to success.

Less than six months after concluding the Munich Agreement, Hitler broke it by having the Army occupy the remaining Czech part of Czechoslovakia on 15 March 1939. Slovakia declared itself independent and became a German satellite.[27] Britain and France determined to accept no more German "revisions" and made ready to oppose Germany militarily on the next occasion. Hitler furnished it by demanding that Poland relinquish Danzig and the Corridor, the territory separating German East Prussia from Germany. Hitler did not want these public demands satisfied. What he wanted was an opportunity to go to war against a chosen enemy. On 23 May 1939, he told the chief commanders of the Army, Navy, and Air Force that a solution to the living space question was not possible without the invasion of foreign states. Danzig was not the object, but the expansion of living space in the East. Poland would always be an enemy. Hitler had therefore made the "decision to attack Poland at earliest convenient opportunity."[28] A pact with Stalin was concluded on 23 August 1939, providing for the division of Poland between Germany and Russia and guaranteeing Hitler a free hand against Poland.[29]

German armies crossed the German-Polish border on 1 September 1939.[30] In the following days Britain, France, and a number of Commonwealth countries declared war on Germany: Britain, France, Australia, and New Zealand on 3 September, South Africa on 6 September, and Canada on 9 September.[31] They could not save Poland. It became apparent that Hitler and Stalin had agreed on more than the division of Poland. Not only did the Red Army invade and occupy eastern Poland on 17 September, while Polish armies were still resisting the German onslaught, but the Soviet Union also concluded "assistance" treaties with Estonia, Latvia, and Lithuania. The Hitler-Stalin Pact had relinquished these countries to the Soviet "sphere of influence," and they were now occupied by the Red Army with unbelievable barbarity. Finland, which refused to accept Russian conditions, was attacked by the Soviet Union on 30 November 1939 and forced to cede territory in the Peace of Moscow signed on 12 March 1940.

Hitler meanwhile ordered the German Armed Forces to prepare for an attack against France. Neither France nor Britain seemed inclined to accept Hitler's "peace offers." They refused to let him keep what he had or to give him a free hand for more conquests in the east. Germany's attack in the west had to be postponed several times because of poor weather and insufficient preparations. As Britain appeared to move to assist Finland and to prevent German ships from using Norwegian territorial waters for iron ore shipments from Sweden, Hitler became apprehensive about his northern flank and the iron ore supplies. He ordered the occupation of Denmark and Norway, which began on 9 April 1940.

On 10 May 1940, the German armies invaded the Netherlands, Belgium, and France. The Netherlands and Belgium capitulated later in May, and an armistice with France was concluded on 22 June. A British force of some 200,000 was partially encircled at Dunkirk but escaped across the English Channel. The defeat of France and the destruction of the French Army changed the military balance of the world.

Next, Hitler tried to drive Britain out of the war by a major air offensive and the threat of invasion. Hitler's campaign against Britain was somewhat half-hearted. The German Air Force could not defeat the British air defenses, and an invasion across the Channel was apparently not contemplated in earnest. The German submarine offensive against Britain inflicted serious losses, but it was blunted by the British fleet and by American naval support, which only stopped short of outright entry into the war. German-Italian efforts to dominate the Mediterranean Sea and North Africa were similarly unsuccessful.

Even before the air offensive against Britain had reached its greatest intensity, Hitler ordered preparations for an attack against the Soviet Union. While the German preparations were proceeding, Hitler had his Foreign Minister negotiate with the Russian Foreign Minister, Vyacheslav Mihailovich Molotov, about a further division of spheres of influence in southeastern Europe.[32] An Italian invasion of Greece in October 1940 and political upheavals in Yugoslavia in March 1941 caused the German southern flank to turn soft, drawing Germany into a Balkan campaign in the spring of 1941 which delayed the attack against the Soviet Union.

The German attack on Russia began on 22 June 1941. It was accompanied, on Hitler's orders, by a campaign of mass murder against the political infrastructure of the Soviet Union and against approximately five million Jews in Russia and in eastern Europe. These measures had been long in preparation. Hitler had already showed his hand in the anti-Jewish pogrom of 1938. There is general agreement on two of their aspects: the extermination policy was impossible without Hitler as the central factor, and there was a large degree of cooperation on the part of German and non-German individuals and agencies who became involved in the process, in most cases involuntarily.[33]

The start of the Second World War in September 1939 was coupled with a so-called euthanasia program which turned out to be the preparatory stage for the mass murder of Jews in the camps. In Poland, the German troops were followed by special SS and police units who conducted large-scale shootings of intellectuals, priests, partisans, and Jews—just as Hitler had threatened in a speech to senior military commanders in August 1939.[34] At the end of the military campaign, after protests by certain senior Army commanders, the killings were scaled down and conducted in a more "regular" manner, under the pretext of sabotage or espionage.

The campaign against the Soviet Union, however, opened up new possibilities, and this time the preparations for mass killings, particularly of Jews, were more elaborate. The mass killings were introduced in ways designed to mute protests from the regular Army. For one thing, they were carried out in rear areas placed under the authority of SS and police commanders. The commanders of the Einsatzgruppen and Einsatzkommandos (mobile killing groups and squads) operating behind the front still encountered difficulties, but they received a surprising amount of cooperation. The technical preparations for mass killings in camps had been advanced in the euthanasia program; its personnel was now transferred to the camp program for exterminating Jews; and the euthanasia program as a separate operation was ordered phased out. The crucial orders for what became known as the Holocaust were given by Hitler, Himmler, Göring, and Heydrich during the period June–September 1941.[35] Hundreds of thousands of other people were shot as "partisans."

The German military commanders, engaged in battle in a vast foreign land, did not try to stop the killings. The huge rear areas in Russia were thinly controlled by German forces; enormous territories had been traversed but not occupied. The concern of German military commanders was to control these areas so that supply trains would not be blown off the tracks. Even if the military commanders had been unusually sensitive to what the SS, police, and locally recruited militia were doing, they could not have concerned themselves with it very much.

The great majority of the Jews who were killed during the war died in six special death camps in Poland and in the Ukraine. According to the best available estimates, there died at Chelmno, from December 1941 to March 1943, 150,000 Jews; at Belzec, from the winter of 1941–1942 to the spring of 1943, 550,000 Jews; at Sobibor, from April to June 1942 and March to August 1943, 200,000 Jews; at Treblinka, from July 1942 to October 1943, 750,000 Jews; at Oswiecim (Auschwitz), from September 1941 to 28 November 1944, 1,000,000 Jews; and at Majdanek, from October 1942 to October 1943 an estimated 200,000 people, at least 50,000 of them Jews. Those killed by the mobile death squads, in other open-air shootings, and in gas wagons behind the eastern front numbered 1,300,000. Over 800,000

Jews were killed through ghettoization and general privation. About 250,000 Jews were killed by other mistreatment, in camps with smaller killing operations, and in some Rumanian and Croatian camps where large-scale massacres were carried out by a local militia. The total number of Jews killed came to at least 5,050,000.

The German attack against the Soviet Union was successful until October 1941. Advance units reached the outskirts of Moscow. Then the attack collapsed, mired in early rains, frost, and snows in November and December.

After Japan had attacked the United States on 7 December 1941, Hitler declared war on the United States. He evidently hoped for a victory over the Soviet Union while the United States was heavily committed in the Pacific Ocean. But he failed to achieve his victory in the east, and the United States proved to have enough resources for serious commitments in both the Pacific Ocean and the Atlantic Ocean.[36] The year 1942 ended with the disaster of Stalingrad, where the entire German Sixth Army was annihilated and close to 100,000 German soldiers were taken prisoner. The beginning of 1943 found the German Africa Corps in an untenable position, and by May the failure of German naval forces to prevent the United States from supplying Britain across the Atlantic was clear.

In spite of huge efforts by the German military forces and the home front, and in spite of constant increases in arms production, Germany was fighting on too many fronts to force a decision at any of them. The Africa Corps went into captivity in May 1943. A massive German offensive at Kursk in Russia failed in the summer of 1943. By July 1944 the German Army Group Center in Russia was routed, in a catastrophe worse than Stalingrad, with 300,000 men lost, and Red Army units had come within a few miles of the German eastern border. American and British forces built up a growing superiority on the high seas and in the air. Italy, Germany's only major ally in Europe, fell into disorder in July 1943, when Mussolini was overthrown by an internal revolt, and in September Italy changed sides in the war. Germany had one more front to defend.

In June 1944, the Western Allies mounted their long-awaited invasion of France. The Allies occupied Paris in August and reached the Rhine by autumn. The numbers of German losses in the last nine months of the war—approximately 2.7 million dead of a total for the war of approximately 7 million—tell a story of hard fighting and of horror.[37] The Germans' desperate Ardennes offensive of December 1944 to January 1945 could not succeed against the overwhelming Allied military forces and material being brought against Germany.

Hitler knew the war was lost. He had known on a rational level since December 1941, when his Blitzkrieg (lightning-speed war) strategy failed in Russia, that only some sort of "miracle," such as a superior weapon or the internal collapse of Russia, could give him victory.[38] In the deepest recesses of his mind, he perhaps never expected to win but was driven to repeat the traumatic experience of the First World War.[39] He could not capitulate; he could not make peace, as no power would grant him terms; and he refused to give up and remove himself. As a demonic gambler, he continued the war for years, with profound disregard for "his" nation and for the lives he destroyed, hoping against hope for some turn in his fortunes. To the very end he pursued his obsession that he must destroy the Jews. Finally, as the Red Army was closing in on his Reich Chancellery bunker in the center of Berlin, Hitler took his own life. The Nazi propaganda maintained that the Führer had fallen while fighting in the Battle of Berlin. The truth was that the imposter had absconded. He had ended his life as a gambler.

Part Two

The Resistance

Forces of Opposition 4

There were no reliable methods in Germany for measuring popular approval of the government during the period from 1933 to 1945. There is evidence, however, of fluctuations in public opinion.[1] The first Reichstag elections in March 1933 brought the Nazi Party less than half of the popular vote. Approval seems to have increased up to the time of the Sudeten crisis, and it decreased sharply during the crisis. Disapproval of policies leading to war remained strong in the period between the Sudeten crisis and the outbreak of war. During the war years, reasons to support the leadership were entwined with reasons to disapprove of it. On the whole, at all times from 1933 to 1945 the majority of German voters, indeed of the entire population, supported the government, albeit with varying degrees of willingness.

This phenomenon is a common one, even in cases of a criminal regime, but Germany's historical situation contributed to it. The democratic system of the Weimar Republic had not had time to make itself generally accepted and popular. At the end of the Great War the Emperor and the chief military commanders had fled to avoid extradition as "war criminals," leaving the Republic with the odium of fulfilling the peace treaty. It was burdened with ruinous reparations obligations and with a foreign occupation for which the enforcement of payments was only a pretext. It was burdened with the social disruptions caused by a grotesquely inflated currency. Stabilization of the democratic government was nevertheless proceeding when the worldwide economic depression cut it short. From 1930 onward, the parliamentary system failed, to be replaced gradually by semidictatorial caretaker cabinets under presidential emergency authority. Hitler's appointment was a quality leap, but that was not clear until later. Broad acceptance of Hitler's regime was possible also because so many Germans got their nationalism confused with National Socialism, not surprisingly in view of the national humiliations that the country had undergone since 1918. Hitler knew how to foster resentments and to exploit the already widespread refusal to grant legitimacy to the Republic. He was able at the same time to disguise his own lethal obsessions as a concern for national honor. After 1933, the other governments in the world accepted Hitler's, and any who disapproved of it did not show it. Germans could hardly disagree with national renewal when the rest of the world approved of it.

German Resistance to the Nazi government was a direct response to its fundamental injustice and destructiveness. Arbitrariness, criminality, dictatorial oppression, police excesses, persecution of religious leaders and political opponents, and the persecution of so-called non-Aryans (Jews and Gypsies) and the frivolous unleashing of another war—these were the principal causes of the Resistance. For many, the persecution of the Jews was the most important single factor.

The terms "resistance" and "resistance movement" were used in leaflets issued by a group of students and a university professor, called the "White Rose," whose goal was to arouse a people's opposition to the regime. The members of the group were beheaded in Munich in February and March 1943.[2] After the Second World War the terms they used gained currency in German usage, particularly through analogy with the French Résistance.

Resistance both waned and grew in phases. In the first few months after 30 January 1933, the old forms and methods of political debate continued to some extent. A number of newspapers and literary periodicals carried on as before until they were suppressed; political parties disappeared only gradually;

people understood only gradually the price of free speech—concentration camp or prison. In short, a good deal of the early opposition represented a continuation, by sheer momentum, of what had been customary. But all this verbal opposition remained ineffective, and within a few months it was muted.

The next phase of opposition was the underground phase. Its early period overlapped with the gradual suppression of overt opposition during the first two years of the regime. The natural forces of opposition to National Socialism—the trade unions, the Social Democrats, and the Communists—were not united. Social Democrats and Communists were more sharply opposed to each other than they were to the Nazis. It was not until the meeting of the Communist International in Brussels in 1935 that "popular fronts" of Social Democrats and Communists were declared orthodox. By then, the most favorable time for opposition had been lost. When the Nazis still might have been prevented from seizing power, only a small group among the Left was prepared for underground opposition, namely Walter Löwenheim's Marxist Leninist Organization. Löwenheim had founded the organization before 1933 to influence, renew, and if possible control along Marxist Leninist lines the entire socialist movement. After all opposition groups became illegal in 1933, this organization managed to survive underground longer than any other left-wing organization. Through a pamphlet, *Neu beginnen!* (New beginning), produced in Czechoslovakia under the pseudonym Miles, the group became widely known.[3]

There existed an unknown number of opposition groups including conservative, socialist, and Communist ones. If a "group" is defined as consisting of two or more members, an estimated one thousand socialist and Communist groups were active in 1935 and 1936, based on police statistics of arrests and underground leaflet distribution.[4] The estimate for conservative groups is lower but certainly above two hundred. Most of the larger underground organizations were destroyed by the political police early in Hitler's dictatorship. The Miles group, for example, was hit several times by police actions, and by 1938 it became inactive. In the years before the war, the leaders of the broken-up groups either went into exile or were given long terms in penitentiaries or concentration camps. Those who were released from prison remained under police surveillance and could not keep up many contacts. When Austria and Czechoslovakia were annexed in 1938 and 1939, the Left lost its familiar safe havens, where German was spoken. When the Soviet Union concluded its pact with Hitler for the partition of Poland in 1939, members of the Left lost their illusions about the socialist Great Power. The Communists particularly remained largely inactive until Hitler attacked the Soviet Union in 1941.

Dozens of left-wing groups managed to reorganize underground. Some carried out courageous sabotage operations. Because of the conspiratorial methods of those groups, the Gestapo infiltrated them relatively easily. This was the fate, for example, of the Markwitz Circle, a group of Social Democrats, in May 1935 after an informer had wormed his way into their courier service.[5]

Josef (Beppo) Römer, a veteran of the First World War and former commander of the Free Corps "Oberland," organized new anti-Nazi groups every time he was released from arrest. After being held in Dachau Concentration Camp from 1934 to 1939, he again organized Resistance cells during the war. Most of these were Communist or other working-class groups. The most important of them was Robert Uhrig's, the Robby Group, located in the Berlin Osram works which produced light bulbs. This group had been organized underground for espionage for the Soviet Union and at the start of hostilities in June 1941 became active as a part of the war organization of Soviet military intelligence. Römer also provided a link to nationalist-Communist Free Corps veterans who favored cooperation with the Soviet Union during and after the war. Several other groups were involved in this "alliance," such as one led by Walter Budeus, an engine fitter. Römer's final arrest occurred in February 1942. Some 150 other people were involved in his trial, and he and over a hundred others were executed.[6]

One of the best-known Resistance groups, within the Red Orchestra organization, so named by the Gestapo from the jar-

gon word "musician" for Morse code operators, and also connected with Römer, was led by Lieutenant Harro Schulze-Boysen
in the Aviation Ministry. The group operated as the principal
war organization of Soviet espionage. Most of its members
were arrested and tried, and virtually all of its members who
were tried were executed in 1942 and 1943.[7]

All of this resistance was impressive, yet it was too isolated
to be effective. The phenomenon of a determined but largely
ineffective resistance was made up of a variety of forms of
behavior, from semipublic gestures to direct antigovernment
activity at the highest level. Something took place that could be
termed "popular resistance," but it was not "popular" in quantitative terms. Opposition behavior could consist in a refusal to
offer the "German greeting" ("Heil Hitler"). Many paid with
their lives for such a refusal, or for remarks to the effect that
the war was not going well.[8] A refusal to contribute even a small
amount of money to a Nazi fund drive was another method of
opposition used by persons who were unwilling to compromise.
Ewald von Kleist-Schmenzin, a wealthy farmer, told the Nazi
Party District Leader in 1933 that he was an enemy of the party;
he would neither say "Heil Hitler" nor show the swastika flag
nor give money to the party, not even a token ten pennies. This
was early in Hitler's reign, and Kleist had a social standing that
permitted him to risk a good deal with impunity. But he remained equally uncompromising throughout. He was hanged
for his opposition in 1945.[9]

Resistance by working-class groups often manifested itself
in antigovernment leaflet campaigns. This was considered high
treason and punishable by prison term or death. In 1936, the
Gestapo counted 1,643,000 leaflets that had been distributed
illegally.

Resistance also took the form of aiding Jews and others to
escape from the country. One of the most active Resistance
centers in Germany was formed by Hans von Dohnanyi, a former Reich Supreme Court counselor who did war service in
the military intelligence (Abwehr); his superior, Colonel Hans
Oster; Reverend Dietrich Bonhoeffer, a Confessing Church leader

now serving in the Abwehr in "internal emigration" (military service to avoid arrest or conflict with Nazi agencies); and Josef Müller, an opposition Catholic lawyer who also served in the Abwehr. All carried on Resistance activities under the protection of Admiral Wilhelm Canaris, the Abw hr chief. They organized an underground railroad for Jews to escape from Germany and thereby avoid deportation to a death camp in 1941 and 1942. The Gestapo and SD (Security Service) of the SS got wind of the railroad, and they managed, half inadvertently, to destroy the conspiracy group in the Abwehr. Dohnanyi, Oster, and Bonhoeffer were hanged in April 1945.[10]

Resistance was expressed as well through sabotage in factories, the Armed Forces, and against railway lines.[11] A number of opponents of the regime attempted to sabotage, prevent, or shorten the war by informing foreign governments of the projected dates for an attack against their countries. Oster was the best known among those whose sense of duty to their country and to mankind moved them to act in this way.[12]

The churches were organizations of some independence, and from Hitler's point of view, they were ideologically (theologically) oriented and programmed. There were several hundred nationalist and pro-Nazi churchmen in the Lutheran, Reformed, and Catholic churches. Socialists among the clergy were relatively rare. The churches were preoccupied with preaching the Gospels and performing pastoral service. The clergy did not tend to oppose the government politically, unless their activities in their primary field of concern were curtailed intolerably. But there were many in the churches who considered this to be the case in Nazi Germany. The Confessing Church of the Lutheran and Reformed faiths was formed in opposition to the attempt to Nazify the Protestant churches, for the purpose of protecting purely religious activities. There was individual, heroic resistance in the churches—from priests, nuns, ministers, and a few prelates and bishops. Pastor Martin Niemöller is a shining example. He challenged the Nazis and told the Gestapo agents detailed to sit in his Berlin-Dahlem parish congregation to get down accurately every word he said. He was put in a concentration camp in 1937, from which he was not liberated until 1945. But as institutions, the churches were no threat to the regime. Dietrich Bonhoeffer, a leader in the Confessing Church, found little support even within this organization for his view that you must "open thy mouth for the dumb." He was moved to enter into political, as distinct from religious, opposition, mainly by his concern for the Jews.[13]

Resistance was manifested, finally, in the crime of high treason. There was a conspiracy to stage a coup d'état and secure the overthrow of the Nazi government, which culminated in the assassination attempt against Hitler on 20 July 1944.

There was always resistance, both open and covert, in all social and occupational strata. Thousands gave their lives to the Resistance on guillotines, on gallows, and at execution pits in concentration camps. Resistance by ordinary people without any real leverage on power in the state caused the regime much worry and anxiety. The situation reports of the SD (Sicherheitsdienst, or Security Service) of the Reich Central Security Department (Reichssicherheitshauptamt, RSHA), headed by Heinrich Himmler, Reich Leader of the SS, and by SS generals Heydrich, Heinrich Müller, and Ernst Kaltenbrunner, bear ample witness. Hitler himself referred to these worries about popular opposition frequently during the war. Foreseeing the loss of the war and referring to the unrest of 1918 and 1919, Hitler said on 7 April 1942 at dinner: "If the slightest attempt at a riot were to break out at this moment anywhere in the whole Reich, I'd take immediate measures against it. Here's what I'd do: (a) on the same day, all the leaders of the opposition, including the leaders of the Catholic party, would be arrested and executed; (b) all the occupants of the concentration camps would be shot within three days; (c) all the criminals on our lists—and it would make little difference whether they were in prison or at liberty—would be shot within the same period."[14]

The so-called euthanasia program aroused opposition of a nonpolitical kind because it affected people's family ties with the mentally ill, the feeble, and mongoloid or otherwise handicapped children. Hitler had considerable difficulty getting a program launched to kill off all of these "useless eaters."[15] "Mercy killing" or not, it was murder, and the regime had trouble getting a grip on it in a systematic and organized fashion. The program did not get under way on a massive scale until after the start of the war.

Strong protests to the "euthanasia" program came from Catholic and Lutheran church leaders, notably from Bishops Clemens Count von Galen of Münster and Theophil Wurm of Württemberg. Considering the difficulties in making anything public at all, these protests were certainly vociferous.[16] Hitler ordered the official program suspended on 24 August 1941—at the time when the personnel doing the killing was needed for the projected mass killing of Jews. At least 80,000 to 100,000 "euthanasia" victims had been murdered. The process continued "unofficially" in the concentration camps, where tens of thousands more were murdered. The official suspension was a victory of sorts for the church leaders. They had protested; the program had apparently been halted; and the protesters had not been removed or even restricted in their activities. But the Nazis had also been successful. Hitler wished to deal cautiously with the churches during the war, since their support of the war was valuable to him; after the war, he intended to destroy them.[17] So the Nazis had silenced the church opposition on this issue while continuing with what was left of the project.

It is safe to say that the majority of the German people were opposed to the violent persecution and mass murder of the Jews.[18] Their sense of fundamental justice did not accept such violent outrages as the 1938 pogrom. Judicial and Nazi Party investigations and trials in the wake of the pogrom bear witness to this fact. With regard to his designs against the Jews, Hitler faced a problem similar to the one encountered on 27 September 1938 when he had found the population unwilling to accept a war. He needed a nation willing to support his criminal impulses; but they provoked strong opposition. Just as the November 1938 pogrom had had to be cut short, violent persecution, especially murder, in the future would have to be conducted in utmost secrecy. The reactions of foreign countries were a minor consideration during the war, but the reactions of the German population could be a serious matter. The majority of the German people might have supported, in the first years of Hitler's rule, a certain amount of discrimination against Jews.[19] But a large minority—up to 40 percent—had rejected the physical violence and brutality of the November 1938 pogrom.[20] A similar estimate applies to the rumored wartime shootings of Jews in Poland and Russia. The regime's attempt to keep mass exterminations utterly secret speaks for itself. But it meant also that reaction to the program could only be limited. The Gestapo could gather little information on reactions to death camps and mass gassings, because these were almost unknown.

Nevertheless, a considerable "number of ordinary Germans actually did something for Jews in the face of Hitler's police state"; one careful study cites around three thousand cases.[21] Opposition to the persecution of Jews was strongest in the age groups of forty or older and in the socioeconomic categories of males, white-collar workers at upper levels, and independents. The least active opponents of anti-Jewish measures appear to have been females and blue-collar workers. The Gestapo also found that criticism of and opposition to anti-Jewish measures increased every time the violence against Jews intensified.

Opposition to the lethal aspects of his policies contributed to making Hitler apprehensive of possible attacks on his life. In June 1941, as he launched the attack on the Soviet Union and the ultimate campaign against the Jews, Hitler ordered an injunction against any performances of Friedrich Schiller's *William Tell,* in which an oppressor is assassinated.[22] But Hitler had worried about the possibility of assassination even before launching his war. In 1939, he had discussed with Albert Speer his plans for a new postwar Greater Germanic Reich Chancellery. The Chancellery had to be a fortress with huge steel doors, sliding bullet-proof shutters, and no windows in the facade, except a small balcony at the fifth-story level. Hitler explained to Speer that he might have to take "unpopular measures" some day, and there might be a revolt: "The center of the Reich must be defensible like a fortress."[23]

Popular opposition that was scattered, isolated, and easily controlled by security forces could not destabilize the dictatorship. Courageous acts by opponents barely disturbed the gigantic war machine. This resistance was therefore not effective, since it was incapable of changing the regime. To declare these individual or collective acts of heroism in the struggle against Nazism to have been ineffective is not a judgment on their moral value. Isolated individuals and groups, without hope of being effective, did not make success the criterion for their commitment, any more than did other resistors with better access to the centers of power.

All categories of opposition included representatives of all sociological and political strata, professions, and trades, and of every level of education, income, background, wealth, and influence. There were engineers, skilled workers, farmers, civil servants, diplomats, government ministers, lawyers, Catholic priests, Protestant ministers, housewives, artists, students, researchers, scholars, scientists, academics, soldiers and officers, trade union functionaries, businessmen, and industrialists. The entire political spectrum from Left to Right was represented in the Resistance, from internationalists and world-revolution-minded Communists to conservative politicians and former pillars of throne and altar, even including disillusioned National Socialists.

Varieties of Thought 5

All Resistance groups aimed at the overthrow of Hitler's Nazi dictatorship. All those involved in the Resistance also wished to avoid a restoration of the pre-1933 conditions that had produced the Nazi regime. But beyond this, their views on the political and social reconstruction of Germany after Hitler differed considerably. Concepts for post-Nazi reconstruction ranged from the restoration of the Constitution and the rule of justice, at one end of the scale, to the expropriation of all private wealth, state ownership of the means of production, and the "dictatorship of the proletariat" at the other end.

The Communist program was the familiar one of instituting common ownership of the means of production, a merciless fight against "class enemies," the rule of the Communist Party (no others allowed), and political alignment with the Soviet Union.[1] Peace was usually on the list, although it had a hollow ring after the Soviet attacks on Poland, Finland, Estonia, Latvia, Livonia, and Bessarabia.

The Social Democrats believed that general and equal adult suffrage must lead to a just representation of the interests of the "working classes."[2] They favored the authority of parliament and the central government over decentralized powers that tended to be open to influences from oligarchic, agrarian-patriarchal, clerical, or even monarchist forces. Control of the social security administration was to be transferred to the workers. During the Great Depression, drastic reductions of benefits by the government had been traumatic. Nationalization of key industries was still among the tenets of Social Democracy, but the nationalization of land ownership was abandoned, and state socialism was rejected in principle. Participation in economic decisions at every level, from shops to government, was considered more important than schemes for the redistribution of wealth. Participation could be effective only if it was informed, so that education was stressed as a major issue.

Two principal socialist leaders emerged in the Resistance. One was Julius Leber, a reserve officer who had received the Iron Cross First Class in the First World War, Reichstag Deputy in the 1920s, and defense expert, who spent years in Nazi concentration camps and then went "underground" by becoming a coal merchant. The other leader was Wilhelm Leuschner, a trade union leader, former interior minister in the state government of Hesse, and concentration camp veteran. Leber insisted on a "purely socialist solution" for the reorganization of Germany after Hitler's fall, without expressing particular interest in a democratic solution or the revival of the political parties. He favored toleration in religious and racial matters, "restoration of the rights of Jews," equality of rights for the sexes, abolition of the death penalty, and methods of punishment aiming at resocialization instead of retribution.

Leber and Leuschner both insisted on the national unity of the labor movement, particularly the trade unions. They were opposed by another prominent socialist, Carlo Mierendorff, a former Secretary General of the Transport Workers' Union, former Reichstag deputy, and veteran of concentration camps, who wanted factory unions instead of trade unions. But all three wanted the unions to become, in the words of Leuschner, "a real political instrument of the German worker." They accepted delegates from the white-collar and Christian labor organizations, namely Max Habermann and Jakob Kaiser, but they disagreed with them on cultural and school issues. Kaiser wanted to keep denominational schools where they existed; Leber and Leuschner wanted nine years of compulsory attendance for all children in the same type of standardized, nondenominational, nonreligious schools. Mierendorff and another Social Democrat leader, Professor Adolf Reichwein, favored cooperation with the Communists; Leuschner and Leber objected.

Reichwein, Mierendorff, and later also Leuschner and Leber collaborated in Helmuth Count von Moltke's Kreisau Circle. The Kreisau Circle was made up of resistors who agreed that the Hitler regime was bound to collapse and that a representative cross-section of anti-Nazi German society should prepare plans for reconstruction and be ready to serve. The group held major meetings in July 1941, May and October 1942, and June 1943.[3] Some of the larger meetings were held at Moltke's Kreisau estate, but most of the others took place in Berlin. The group also included Peter Count Yorck von Wartenburg, a lawyer and civil servant; Horst von Einsiedel, an economist and Social Democrat; Carl Dietrich von Trotha, a lawyer, economist, and Christian socialist; Adolf Reichwein, a historian, economist, political scientist, and Social Democrat; Professor Hans Peters, a jurist affiliated with the Center Party; Hans Lukaschek, a lawyer, civil servant, Governor of Upper Silesia, and Catholic conservative; Theodor Steltzer, a General Staff officer, civil servant, and pro-socialist; Adam von Trott zu Solz, a lawyer in the foreign service and socialist; Hans Bernd von Haeften, a lawyer in the foreign service and member of the Confessing Church; Harald Poelchau, a Protestant minister in the Berlin-Tegel prison and Christian socialist; Father Augustin Rösch, a regional prefect of the Jesuit Order in Munich; Alfred Delp, a theologian, sociologist, and editor; Theo Haubach, a Social Democrat; Eugen Gerstenmaier, a Protestant theologian and church administrator; Paulus van Husen, a lawyer, civil servant, and Catholic conservative; and Father Lothar König, a theologian and church administrator. A number of other people were associated with the group and participated in the discussions.[4]

The Kreisau group stressed Christianity as the basis of society. They wanted the state to protect the right to work and to own property and to guarantee the daily requirements of "food, clothing, housing, a garden and health." They wanted social units, such as factories, federal states, and municipalities, to be small enough to be manageable. There were to be direct elections at the parish and district levels. At the state and Reich levels, elected representatives and officeholders were to be chosen indirectly, through parish and district councils. State legislatures would elect Reichstag deputies, only half of whom could be chosen from the ranks of state legislators. The first parliament was to be formed without the participation of political parties, only through the election and delegation of individuals from regional and municipal representative assemblies. The Reichstag was not to choose a Chancellor, only to ratify the choice of the Reich Regent (Head of State), who was to be chosen by the parliament. The cabinet ministers required approval by the Reich Regent and the Chancellor, but not by the Reichstag. To ensure that a Chancellor and his cabinet did not stay in power indefinitely with the backing of the Regent, the Reichstag had the opportunity to request the Chancellor's dismissal—but had to agree on a new Chancellor at the same time. This procedure became known as a "constructive vote of no confidence" and was written into the Constitution of the Federal Republic of Germany in 1949. All of the proposals of the Kreisau Circle aimed at avoiding both a revival of the conditions of the Weimar Republic which had produced the Nazi dictatorship and a continuation of Nazi rule through uninhibited license of political forces.

Moltke and many of his friends believed they must seek a new spiritual integration of society on the basis of Christianity and must overcome the divisions of class, religion, and political persuasion. Mass population centers were considered threats to a dignified human life; the antidote seemed to be a revitalization of social life based on the family and on small groups and communities. These views owed much to the extreme isolation in which they had been produced.

Seven members of the Kreisau Circle were hanged for their participation in the 20 July 1944 conspiracy: Yorck, Reichwein, Trott, Haeften, Delp, Haubach, and Leber. Mierendorff was killed in an air raid. Moltke was hanged, although his involvement in the conspiracy could not be proven, for having thought and talked about a non-Nazi Germany.

Carl Goerdeler was regarded by many as the chief underground opposition leader.[5] He was a conservative liberal, in close contact with the Kreisau Circle on his left and with opposition personalities like Ulrich von Hassell and Johannes Popitz on his right. His stature and influence in the Resistance, however, fluctuated through the years.

Goerdeler was the Mayor of Leipzig in 1930–1937 and Reich Price Commissioner in 1931–1932 and 1933–1934. He resigned as Mayor when, in his absence, his deputy, who was a Nazi, removed the Mendelssohn monument in front of the Leipzig Gewandhaus. For Goerdeler, this was an issue of principle as much as an issue of authority. He had refused to hoist the swastika flag in 1933, and during the 1 April 1933 "boycott" he had personally protected Jewish businessmen against looting by the SA. Robert Bosch, the opposition industrialist, and others provided funds for Goerdeler to travel abroad and to exhort whomever he met in positions of power to resist Hitler while there was still time. But because Goerdeler was a patriot and a nationalist, many of his views concerning revision of the Treaty of Versailles appeared similar to Hitler's demands. During the war he campaigned for years to form a high-level military pressure group to force Hitler to resign.

Goerdeler produced lengthy reports on economic conditions and proposals for their remedy, on international relations, on administrative issues, and on the reorganization of the German government after Hitler. The recurring themes in these reports were liberty, truth, and good government; the replacement of propaganda and party indoctrination by education; and the necessity for religious instruction. A well-governed state, in Goerdeler's view, was built from the ground up, on the principle of self-government. Goerdeler wanted direct popular elections at the municipal and parish levels. The resulting assemblies were to elect district assemblies. These assemblies would elect state and regional assemblies. These in turn would elect one-half of the Reichstag deputies, the other half to be elected by direct popular vote. There was to be an upper house in the form of a Reich Chamber of Corporations (Reichsständehaus), chosen by neither general suffrage nor delegation from elected bodies. This upper house was to consist of the leaders of industry, commerce, churches, universities, and trade unions.

Since elections would not be possible before demobilization and a government and Head of State were needed immediately, the first Head of State was to be nominated by the government and elected by the upper house. As in the Kreisau Circle's proposals, the Chancellor's cabinet would not depend on Reichstag support, but Goerdeler also proposed that the Head of State could be required by a two-thirds majority of Reichstag deputies or by a combined simple majority of the Reichstag and the Reich Chamber of Corporations to dismiss the cabinet and to appoint a new one at the same time. The government would have authority over legislation. The Reichstag and the Chamber of Corporations could cancel legislation through methods similar to those adopted for a change of cabinet. Again, as in the case of the Kreisau proposals, these were influenced by the emergency situation in which they were drafted, as well as by the circumstances in which they were to come into effect. In a proposal written in 1944, Goerdeler assigned more responsibilities and powers to labor organizations and proposed to nationalize mineral resources, such as iron ore and coal. Goerdeler was arrested, tried, and hanged after 20 July 1944 for his part in the conspiracy.

Somewhat to the right of Goerdeler was Hassell, a former German Ambassador in Rome and son-in-law of Admiral Alfred von Tirpitz.[6] Like Goerdeler, Hassell became an opponent of the Nazis well before the war. From 1939 on, he was deeply involved in the conspiracies to overthrow the regime. In January and February 1940, Hassell drafted a plan for a new government, partly based on discussions with Goerdeler; General Ludwig Beck; Professor Johannes Popitz, Prussian Minister of Finance; Professor Jens Peter Jessen, a political scientist in the Army General Staff during the war; and Erwin Planck, a State Secretary in the Reich Chancellery before Hitler's appointment.

Hassell's plan declared that the "old," 1914 Reich borders with Poland must be assured, that a reduced Poland must be restored, and that Russia must keep her acquisitions of 1939. The program stressed a return to liberty, justice, the rule of law, and respect for human life and for minorities. Hassell offered no details on the structure of future governments or on electoral processes, but he presumed the existence of a government and Regency following the coup d'état. His plan was designed for the emergency situation following the fall of Hitler. The Armed Forces were to take an oath of loyalty to the Regency, and the military commanders were to have full executive powers, so that there would be a temporary military dictatorship during the period immediately after a coup. There were no later proposals from Hassell's pen, but his diary entries show how his estimates of what was politically possible changed in the course of the war, particularly in the face of Allied intentions toward Germany and the deterioration of Germany's military position.[7] Hassell was hanged for his part in the 20 July 1944 conspiracy.

Farther on the Right was Popitz, who drafted a detailed preliminary constitution during the years from 1938 to 1943.[8] He stressed the restoration of the rule of law, "good morals," "a way of life worthy of a human being," individual liberty, protection of property, Christianity as the basis of German life, and the obligation to defend Germany and to behave in ways that violated neither communal interests nor German honor. He described the Wehrmacht as an indispensable institution in the geographic situation of Germany and as a tool for the education and the spiritual and moral rebirth of the nation. The constitution provided for states of approximately equal size, with Prussia making the greatest sacrifice by allowing itself to be reduced to the projected average. The states were to have self-government in many respects, but executive power would be delegated by the central Reich government only for administrative purposes. The result would have been a unitary state structure similar to the French model. The government, in consultation with the Head of State, retained full powers of legislation. There was no provision for a parliament, only for a state council, nominated by the government and appointed by the Head of State, which was to "represent the people in its entirety, until the consolidation of general conditions of the German people's life will permit the formation of a representation of the people on a broad basis." The constitution concluded: "The deep corruption of public life makes necessary the imposition of martial law until further notice, and the transferral of executive power to the armed forces." All those in office before this draft constitution became law were to be removed—Reich and state ministers, undersecretaries, governors, presidents of government agencies, chiefs of police, and all unqualified persons in the civil service without regard to party affiliation. The Nazi Party, the Gestapo, and the concentration camps were to be dissolved. Passages in laws and ordinances discriminating against Jews were to be suspended "pending a definitive disposition."

Berthold, Alexander, and Claus Count von Stauffenberg did not fit easily into a Left-Right scheme. Their concepts on internal and external reorganization were less developed than those of the older co-conspirators. But the Stauffenbergs belonged somewhere to the right of Center.

The Stauffenberg brothers initially accepted as sound much of the Nazi program: the leadership principle based on expertise and authority; a naturally ranked social order; Volksgemeinschaft, or national community, based on the principle of the common good before individual gain; opposition to corruption; emphasis on agricultural life; opposition to the big cities; concepts of race or a pure nationhood; and the determination to have a new, German legal system. But they came to reject the Nazi tenets as the regime turned what they viewed as its positive ideas into their opposites.[9]

The Stauffenbergs were concerned above all to "save the Reich." Berthold Count von Stauffenberg, a jurist, international law specialist, and judge in the Naval High Command, presumably had a realistic expectation of the power relations that would prevail at the end of a war lost by Germany. His younger brother, Claus, a General Staff Colonel, was also not given to illusions concerning the immediate future. But the brothers treasured an image of the greatness of Germany, hidden temporarily, but destined to re-emerge one day in splendor. This image apparently had no reference to specific frontiers. The Stauffenberg brothers' concept of a German Empire owed more to the statesmanship of Emperor Otto I and Emperor Frederick II than to that of Bismarck.[10]

The Stauffenbergs aimed to base Germany's internal renewal on a true community of the people—Volksgemeinschaft—as opposed to the perverted community of the Nazis. Hitler had conceived of Volksgemeinschaft merely as a means to harness the forces of the nation, through the illusion of common interests, for an allegedly necessary struggle for survival, conquest, and ultimate domination. The Stauffenbergs believed that the true common interests of the nation were self-evident, that they must be sought in peace and within a stable social order, and that they could be assured through the "natural" leadership of a highly educated, intellectual elite.

The practical meaning of this idea was rather vague. But the Stauffenbergs were not in a position to produce policy papers. Their views merely placed them in the political landscape. But after a successful revolt, more essentially political forces would have come to bear. The bewilderment resulting from the experience of a self-destructive multiparty system in the Weimar Republic and the extreme cultural isolation of German patriots in the Nazi police state explained in part the brothers' apparent neglect of the practical side of securing the ideals to which they subscribed.

The Stauffenberg brothers referred to the "natural ranks" of human society that must be respected, as well as to "suitable forces" for governing the land, which were to come from all strata of society, according to a person's intellectual and moral qualification. They rejected what they called "dishonest egalitarianism" and the denial of genetic and social heredity, and they wished people to find sufficiency and fulfillment in their respective occupations and environments. No one was to be excluded from political participation, but the Stauffenbergs wondered whether there might not be better ways for attaining these ideals than the mechanisms of political parties. The Stauffenbergs thought of representatives as possibly emerging from communities and occupational associations, such as those of manufacturers, employers, workers, and professionals, in a sort of syndicalist system, not dissimilar to the ideas of the Kreisau Circle.

Military Involvement   6

Whereas the Resistance was representative of all German society in sociological, economic, and political terms, it was not representative in quantitative terms, like an unofficial parliament. Broad support, actual or potential, among the population was lacking for the actions of the Resistance as well as for its ideas.

There were three main reasons for the lack of broad support for the Resistance. First, most Germans accepted Hitler's government as duly constituted and properly legal. They shared this position with the Vatican; the governments of Britain, France, Italy, the United States, and the Soviet Union; the organizers of the 1936 Olympic Games; the chairmen of foreign veterans' organizations; members of the British royal family; internationally famous explorers and scholars; and other prominent private and semiofficial persons. In 1938, during the Sudeten crisis, Prime Minister Neville Chamberlain refused to accede to secret requests from the German Resistance to refuse Hitler's demands so that the dictator might be overthrown for irresponsibly starting a new war. Chamberlain explained his refusal by comparing the German opposition with the supporters of James II who had been driven out of England in the Glorious Revolution of 1688—those "Jacobites" had wanted to overthrow William III of Orange and to put James II on the English throne.[1]

Another reason for the lack of widespread support for the Resistance was the success of Hitler's government. It had re-

stored order, overcome unemployment, restored a credible defensive capacity, and achieved large territorial revisions of the
Treaty of Versailles. Later, Hitler's government also appeared
to be having success in a war that was regarded by great numbers
of Germans as having been forced upon Germany. Setbacks in
that war did not begin to unfold on any significant scale until
1942. Even in 1943 and 1944, these setbacks did not seem
irreversible. When the government's control began to break down
in 1944 and 1945, the loyalty of the population to their political
and military leadership still suffered only marginally. The general population felt threatened not so much by the policies of
the regime as by the Allied air raids, the advance of the Allied
armies in the east and west, and the prospect of an Allied military
occupation. The government's campaigns of murder against the
Poles, Jews, Soviet prisoners-of-war, Jehovah's Witnesses, Gypsies, and other persecuted groups were very secret and little
known, and what was known of them did not seem to threaten
individuals at large if they did not belong to one of the persecuted categories.

The final reason for the absence of broad-based support for
the Resistance was the feeling that the Nazi police state and its
instruments were ubiquitous. In addition to the Gestapo and
the SD, there were innumerable agents, agencies, and informers
of the party, on the provincial level (Gau), the district level
(Kreis), the precinct level (Bezirk), and the block level.

The "natural" opposition to the Nazis, composed of the trade
unions, the Social Democrats, and the Communists, were more
at odds with each other than with the Nazis before Hitler's
appointment as Chancellor, and even afterward. A coalition of
left-wing opponents, or a "popular front," became possible only
when the Communists received directives to this effect and when
the Soviet Union and France formed an alliance in 1935.[2] The
disarray of the left-wing opposition, as well as their conspiratorial methods, made it relatively easy for the Gestapo to infil-
trate and control them.

The Army and its officer corps, however, were largely immune
to Gestapo surveillance and penetration and to the influence of

the Nazi Party. The social fabric of the Army officer corps and its code of ethics left little room for informers, even if such persons had not tended naturally rather to congregate in police organizations. Notwithstanding Hitler's laments after the coup d'état of 20 July 1944 about disloyalty in the Army officer corps, the officer corps was loyal and useful to the dictator.[3] At the same time, the insulation of the officer corps from the Nazi police state made it a haven for many who were threatened for political or "racial" reasons and who chose to go into "internal emigration" through service in the Wehrmacht. This situation was true also, to a smaller degree, of the Navy and the Air Force. The Navy, however, was concerned to live down a revolutionary image dating from 1918. The Air Force was for the most part a new service developed under the aegis of Göring. Given the necessity of an organized armed force for the overthrow of the Nazi state and given the Wehrmacht's exceptional insulation, elements of the Army had to be regarded as the instrument particularly suited for being the arm of a revolt. It remained to find methods of gaining control of sufficient Army elements for this purpose. The greatest obstacle here was the system of military obedience and the oath of loyalty. The most suitable arm for a revolt was also the most conservative and nationalist force in society. No major government has been overthrown in the twentieth century as long as it retained the loyalty of the Army; without the Army, the prospects for the Resistance were poor indeed.

Two major contradictions emerge here. On the one hand, it would not be possible to deploy elements of the Wehrmacht for the overthrow of the government before the elimination of Hitler, the Supreme Commander, because of the obligation of obedience to him. On the other hand, the elimination of Hitler by a systematic and coordinated method could be accomplished, as things stood, only by members of the Armed Forces. Besides Hitler's most loyal henchmen, a few members of the Wehrmacht were almost the only ones with access to his person. Among those placed favorably for an assassination attack, only a handful were willing to carry it out, provided an opportunity could be arranged. As a result, the precondition for a revolt and coup d'état had to be created essentially by the same category of people who were inclined to act against the regime only after the removal of the Supreme Commander. This was like squaring a circle: the status quo of internal power had to be changed before the revolution.

The soldier's oath of loyalty was, of course, more than a mere alibi.[4] In the Wehrmacht, as in all military forces, military obedience was a serious obstacle to individual decisions about the limits of loyalty and about the right or duty to refuse obedience in the face of illegal orders. In war, while facing the enemy, the soldier's feelings of solidarity with his comrades are dominant. A decision to break the oath, to subvert and to act against the supreme military and political leadership, would throw an individual into solitude and isolation from his comrades. Such a decision could not be expected from large numbers of soldiers, only from a few.

There were military men, including some who supported the Resistance, who considered their oath invalid since the leader to whom it had been sworn had broken his oath of office many times over, and still they insisted that they could not act against the regime before the dictator had been killed. Most people see little difference between the assassination of a tyrant and what is commonly termed murder. Most people seem disinclined to kill unless they are given orders sanctioned by society in a time of war. Then they kill designated enemies. Then the question is not one of individual responsibility. The remarkable fact is not that a majority of military men felt inhibited about taking action against their Supreme Commander, but that so many in the Armed Forces were willing to do so.

Events between 1933 and 1938 placed senior military men in opposition to Hitler. Whereas the underground opposition began immediately in political, religious, and other concerned circles after Hitler's appointment in 1933, resistance from the military forces could hardly be expected. President von Hindenburg, the Commander in Chief and (in the public view) hero of the First World War, had appointed the new Chancellor, who was also a veteran of the Great War and a politician who showed extraordinary friendliness toward the Armed Forces. The Chancellor began immediately to expand the Armed Forces, to appropriate funds, to provide new and better equipment and weapons, to bring the Armed Forces up to an internationally current standard.

General Beck was Chief of Troop Office in the Reichswehr Ministry from 1 October 1933; the Troop Office was renamed General Staff of the Army on 1 July 1935, so that Beck's title was afterward Chief of the General Staff of the Army until his resignation became effective on 27 August 1938. He had supported the expansion of the Army but insisted on deliberate and cautious speed in order to avoid international tensions.[5] A German Army of between 300,000 and 400,000 men was reasonable, given that in 1933 Germany was surrounded by alliances in which France had an active armed-forces establishment of 600,000 men plus 900,000 reservists, Poland counted 284,000 in active service with over 900,000 reservists, Czechoslovakia had 110,000 in active service, Yugoslavia had about as many again, Rumania had 246,000, and the Soviet Union had 562,000.[6] Germany had not been allowed to train reservists since the implementation of the Treaty of Versailles in 1921. In the view of both Hitler and the military leadership, the SA was not only not a usable military force but, as an internal danger, was rather an element of weakness.[7]

In the course of the 1930s, Beck became increasingly critical of Hitler's policies. He agreed that Germany was strategically and tactically in a vulnerable position and that certain revisions of the Treaty of Versailles were desirable. But he believed firmly that revisions could and must be accomplished through patient negotiation and that international balance and peace could not be based on threats to other countries and a bid for hegemony. Though he appeared slow to understand Hitler's intentions, he was in a position similar to that of most of his contemporaries. As Hitler's policies developed, Beck was forced to take seriously the dictator's most fantastic statements. Beck criticized them as reckless, perfidious, and conflict-prone. He knew that a war which threatened the vital interests of the other Great Powers could lead only to a more definitive defeat and reduction of Germany than that suffered in the First World War. Beck shared his rejection of war with the chiefs of staff of the armed forces of other major powers. But Beck's position transcended the opportunism that it might suggest. Beck opposed war, whatever the prospects of success or failure, unless it was a clear question of defense against an attack.[8] He agreed with his predecessor, Fieldmarshal Helmut Count von Moltke, in regarding every war, even a victorious one, as a "national disaster."[9]

When Hitler announced his far-reaching policy of territorial expansion on 5 November 1937, Beck was not present.[10] He was informed on 10 November of what had been said, and on 12 November he wrote and filed a scathing indictment of Hitler's statesmanship, citing Hitler's "renewed endangering of the unity of the German people," his "wishful thinking," and "his astounding lack of solid foundations." He wrote: "Policy is the art of the possible. All three of the peoples [Germany, France, and Czechoslovakia] are in the world at the same time, moreover [together] in Europe. This must mean that first of all every possibility for an arrangement is to be exhausted, particularly in view of the relative strengths."[11]

France was Czechoslovakia's principal ally. Beck agreed that the "Czech question," namely the strategic threat posed by Czechoslovakia and by her alliance with France, needed to be settled. Certainly this could be done if the part of Czechoslovakia dominated by a German-speaking, formerly Austrian population were acquired through invoking the right of national self-determination, for much of Czechoslovakia's geographic and military potential was located in a belt along its western border, in the German-speaking region. But Beck expressed his conviction that this ought to be done through diplomatic channels and that a military operation against Czechoslovakia could not be considered except as "an aid," in the strategic sense, in case of a French attack against Germany.[12] No blade is so fine that it can pass between the preparations for defense and attack—they are identical—but the evidence is unequivocal that, for Beck, Germany's preparations were for defense.

Hitler's 5 November 1937 conference led to a crisis in which the War Minister, Fieldmarshal von Blomberg, was disgraced over a mésalliance into which he was apparently goaded by Göring; the Commander in Chief of the Army, Colonel General von Fritsch, was forced to resign on trumped-up charges; and there was a general retirement among senior commanding generals and foreign servants.[13] Hitler then chose to move rapidly concerning the Austrian question.

The desire of the peoples of Austria and Germany after 1918 to live in one state has never been seriously questioned. This desire had been frustrated twice through the dictate of foreign powers, in disregard of the principle of national self-determination.[14] Nevertheless, when Beck had been briefed in May 1937 by his Deputy Chief of Staff, General Erich von Manstein, concerning the prospect of German military intervention in Austria in case of an attempt to restore the Habsburg monarchy there, Beck objected on grounds that such intervention could only destroy any chances for union and that it would plunge Germany into a conflict with France, probably with Czechoslovakia, and also with Britain, Russia, Poland, Lithuania, and even Hungary and Italy. Beck refused flatly to make any plans for a German intervention in Austria.[15]

Beck supported the German-Austrian union itself, but his treatment of the issue was based on his insistence on peaceful, negotiated settlements. When, however, on 10 March 1938 Hitler ordered preparations for an invasion of Austria on 12 March, there were several reasons for Beck to comply: he was given a direct order by the Supreme Commander (in the absence of General von Brauchitsch, who was not in Berlin); the Army was vulnerable because of the unresolved Fritsch affair; Hitler threatened to use SS troops if the Army balked; the Austrian Chancellor, Kurt von Schuschnigg, had announced on 9 March a referendum which was certain to sabotage a German-Austrian union at this time; and the Austrian government had come under

the control of Seyss-Inquart, the Austrian National Socialist
Minister of the Interior and Minister for Security who was to
become Chancellor on 12 March; Seyss-Inquart believed that
military intervention was superfluous since his government was
entirely willing to enter into the union, but alternatively Seyss-
Inquart could be instructed to ask for military "aid." Beck may
not have been aware of all the details of the situation, but he
could see that the moment was favorable to achieve without
bloodshed or international conflict a goal of which he approved.[16]

Beck's dilemma was that a success on the order of the union
of Austria with Germany would increase Hitler's popularity
enormously and would weaken the forces represented by Beck;
but Beck could not prevent that success, even if at his sud-
den confrontation with Hitler on 10 March 1938 he used his
only and ultimate weapon, resignation. His resignation would
neither prevent the union of Austria with Germany nor curtail
Hitler's adventures. On the contrary, Beck would then be unable either to help Fritsch or to avert war with Czechoslovakia
and France.

Beck had resisted Hitler's pressure for aggressive military
plans against Czechoslovakia as soon as they were ordered. On
3 May 1935 he had received a directive to prepare a military
operation against Czechoslovakia; on the next day, he wrote to
the Commander in Chief of the Army, General von Fritsch, that
such a plan could be considered only in the context of a possible
war with France, and not at all for years to come while the
thirty to forty divisions necessary to defend the western frontier
against France were not available. Beck ruled out any attack against
Czechoslovakia at any time, except an operational one designed
as a strategic defensive measure for the German Armed Forces
in case of conflict with a major power.[17] If practical preparations for war were intended, Beck requested to be relieved of
his post.

The question of offensive planning against Czechoslovakia
was still pending when Hitler pressed for action in 1937. His
announcement of territorial conquests on 5 November was fol-

lowed by directives dated 7 and 21 December, ordering preparations for an attack against Czechoslovakia, regardless of whether Germany was threatened or attacked by Czechoslovakia, France, or any other power.[18] The Blomberg-Fritsch affair and the union with Austria intervened before further developments in this matter. Then on 21 April 1938, Hitler ordered General Keitel, the new Chief of OKW, to prepare a surprise attack on Czechoslovakia. Keitel submitted a draft on 20 May. On 28 May, Hitler assembled his senior military commanders and government and Nazi Party officials in the Chancellery to inform them of his "unalterable decision to smash Czechoslovakia by military action within a foreseeable time." On 30 May, a written directive with these words was issued.[19]

On 7 May 1938, Beck had warned his Commander in Chief, General von Brauchitsch, that France and Britain would assist Czechoslovakia against a German attack but that a negotiated solution was possible. Beck supported his arguments with a good amount of military-technical detail. Brauchitsch conveyed to Hitler only the technical arguments, without any of Beck's political points, yet he was rebuffed sharply by Hitler.

On 30 May, Beck read to Brauchitsch a memorandum he had written in response to Hitler's announcement of 28 May regarding military action against Czechoslovakia. Beck repeated his arguments about the relative strength of Germany vis-à-vis its potential opponents. He referred to the virtually inexhaustible overseas resources available to France and Britain: their colonies, dominions, maritime communications, bases. The resources of the United States would be brought in eventually. Beck concluded that if Hitler ordered an attack in the face of these facts, he had been receiving poor advice:

> The Führer's remarks demonstrate once again the total inadequacy of the existing military hierarchy at the highest level. Constant expert counseling by the Supreme Commander of the Wehrmacht on issues of warfare and above all on issues of military combat must be demanded, as well as a clear demarcation and observance of responsibilities. If the brake is not applied here soon, with the object of arriving at a change in conditions that

have become intolerable, and if the present anarchy continues, then the future fate of the Wehrmacht in peace and war and, with it, the fate of Germany can be seen only in the blackest colors.

A further memorandum by Beck, dated 3 June, concentrated on the more purely military aspects of the argument. In the meantime, Beck had ordered an indoor war game to study the course of a German attack on Czechoslovakia based on the assumption of France's intervention against Germany. Beck summed up the results as showing that Czechoslovakia could be defeated in a few weeks, but that meanwhile the French Army would have advanced into Germany and that Germany would not have the strength to stop this advance.[20]

Beck had no personal access to Hitler, and he could address senior commanders only through the Commander in Chief. He kept up his barrage of memoranda to Brauchitsch. On 16 July 1938, Beck reported to the Commander in Chief again, stating: "We are faced with the fact that a German military action against Czechoslovakia would lead automatically to a European or World War . . . which would end most probably not only in a military catastrophe but in a general catastrophe for Germany." Once France and Britain had intervened, they would not aim merely at the restoration of Czechoslovakia but would conduct "a fight to the death against Germany."[21] Beck's memorandum culminated in his insistence that Hitler be forced to abandon his plan: "In the light of my previous statements I regard it as my duty today—in full knowledge of the significance of such a step but conscious of the responsibility laid upon me by my official instructions for the preparation and conduct of a war—to put forward the following urgent request: the Supreme Commander of the Wehrmacht must be induced to halt the war preparations which he has ordered and to postpone his proposed solution by force of the Czech question until the military conditions for it will have changed radically."

The tenor throughout Beck's memoranda was that this change could not occur because France, Britain, the United States, and possibly Russia and other states would come to Czechoslovakia's aid. Germany would never be "ready" for another war, if "ready" meant prepared with a prospect for ultimate success. Beck requested that Brauchitsch "clarify with the senior commanders of the Army all questions [regarding the German intentions to go to war, the various tasks to be assigned, and any objections] before the conference which the Führer intends to hold with the commanding generals, so that a clear and uniform position can be presented to oppose him [the Führer]."

Beck kept to the military sphere in arguing his case. He appealed to Brauchitsch's professional sense and concern for the institution to which they both belonged. But he went so far as to urge a confrontation with Hitler. This move could lead to awkward complications.

Beck explained to Brauchitsch in person on 16 July 1938, reading from prepared notes:

All upright and serious German men in positions of responsibility in the state must feel called upon and duty-bound to employ all conceivable means and ways, including the most extreme, to avert a war against Czecho[slovakia] which in its effects must lead to a world war that would mean *finis Germaniae*. The most senior commanders in the Wehrmacht are called upon and qualified above all others for this task, because the Wehrmacht is the executive instrument of the leadership of the state in the conduct of war. At stake here are ultimate decisions concerning the continued existence of the nation; history will indict these commanders of blood guilt if they do not act according to their professional and political knowledge and conscience. Their soldierly obedience has a limit beyond which their knowledge and their responsibility forbid them to carry out an order. If their advice and warnings in such a situation are not heard, they have the right and the duty before the nation and before history to resign from their posts. If they all act thus with a united will, the execution of an act of war is impossible. Thereby they will have saved their Fatherland from the worst, from ruin. It is a lack of greatness in a soldier in the highest position, and a lack of understanding of his duty, if at such times he sees his duties and tasks only in the restricted confines of his military assignments, without becoming conscious of his supreme responsibility before the entire nation. Extraordinary times demand extraordinary actions! Other upright men in responsible positions in the state outside the Wehrmacht will join in . . . If the intervention of qualified men succeeds in averting a war, considerable domestic tensions will have to be reckoned with . . . It will therefore be necessary, either during or following the intervention, to bring about a decisive showdown between the Wehrmacht and SS.

There can be no doubt that Beck aimed at a coup d'état to overthrow Hitler. As Manstein explained during the Nürnberg trials after the war, a dictator ceases being a dictator if he allows himself to be forced.[22] Beck knew it; Hitler knew it. Hitler could not survive as dictator if the senior commanders confronted him as a group and won.

On 19 July 1938, briefing the Commander in Chief again, Beck provided further details on his request for a collective protest by senior commanders:[23]

It ought to be considered whether this step should be pursued to the point that a showdown with the SS and the party bigwigs becomes inevitable for the reestablishment of orderly conditions of law and justice. Probably for the last time Fate has offered an opportunity to liberate the German nation and the Führer himself from the nightmare of a Cheka and the manifestations of party bigwiggery which influence the mood in the nation and revive Communism and which destroy the continued existence and the welfare of the Reich. The following points of view, inter alia, must be brought to the fore: 1. There can and must be no doubt that this struggle is conducted for the Führer. 2. Upright and capable men of the party must be informed about the seriousness of the situation through objective information; they must be convinced of the necessity of such a step; and they must be won over to it. E.g. Gauleiter Wagner in Silesia, Governor Bürckel in Vienna, the Group Commander in Vienna, and the Commanding General of the Eighth Army Corps (on the occasion of the athletic competitions in Breslau) could be employed for this. Not even the slightest suspicion of any plot must arise, and nevertheless the closest solidarity of the highest military leadership must support this step. Such generals are also to be found in the Air Force. Short, clear slogans: For the Führer! Against the war! Against the tyranny of the party bosses! Peace with the church! Freedom of expression! An end to Cheka methods! Back to the rule of law in the Reich! Reduction of all levies by half! No building of palaces! Housing for the people! Prussian simplicity and decency!

In this proposal there was no pretense of military argument. It was a proposal to end Gestapo terror, tyranny, and arbitrary dictatorship. Beck implied nothing less than the removal of the Nazi system. The slightest suspicion of a plot had to be avoided, because it *was* a plot. "For the Führer" was a propaganda line. In reality the proposal was meant to destroy Hitler's power.

On 29 July 1938, Beck briefed Brauchitsch once more.[24] He urged the Commander in Chief, together with the army group commanders and other commanding generals, to confront the Führer and declare that "they were resigning in a group if the Führer insisted on the prosecution of the war. The form of this declaration cannot be too forceful, hard, and brutal . . . It was foreseen on 16 July 1938 that in any case internal strains had to be expected. Accordingly it will be necessary for the Army to prepare not only for possible war but also for an internal showdown which it should be possible to confine to Berlin. Issue directive accordingly. Get Witzleben together with Helldorf." General Erwin von Witzleben was Commander of the Third Army Corps and Military District III (Berlin); Wolf Heinrich Count von Helldorf was President of Police in Berlin. Beck thought that the moment for a collective protest would come after mid-September. Concrete planning for the coup d'état was now in progress.[25]

The next step had to be a briefing of the senior Army commanders by the Commander in Chief, along the lines urged by his Chief of the General Staff. It transpired that Hitler was proposing to address the army group commanders, commanding generals, and others of similar rank at the Jüterbog training grounds, where he planned to announce the "rehabilitation" of General von Fritsch. This would be an opportunity for the confrontation. In the meantime, Brauchitsch was to convene a briefing of his own, at which he would read to the senior Army commanders a memorandum on the military and political situation prepared by Beck, which concluded that the war plans

must be abandoned and that all generals were unanimous in
their support of this demand. Brauchitsch was to establish whether
all agreed and then to inform the Führer accordingly.[26] He was
to request that the generals take the same position vis-à-vis the
Führer on any future occasions.

Brauchitsch held this briefing on 4 August 1938. But he did
not deliver the presentation prepared for him by Beck. Instead,
he had Beck read to the group his memorandum of 16 July.
Still, this was strong language. The assembled generals were
nearly unanimous in their agreement with Beck's views. Only
two voiced disagreement. Brauchitsch concluded the briefing by
declaring their general agreement in rejecting war, but he did
not request that the generals confront Hitler with a refusal to
carry out orders in case of war, either collectively or singly.[27]
Beck was isolated.

Hitler must have been informed of the briefing. Beck's memorandum of 16 July was circulated as a secret document, and
Brauchitsch transmitted it to Hitler and had a heated exchange
about it with the dictator.[28] Hitler moved to head off the revolt
by summoning the senior chiefs of staff, who were most likely
to have been under Beck's influence, to his Berghof vacation
house on 10 August. Colonel Jodl, Head of the Territorial Defense Section in the OKW, described this meeting in his diary:

> 10 August. The Army chiefs [of staff] and the chiefs [of staff]
> of Air Force Groups, Lieutenant-Colonel Jeschonnek, and I are
> ordered to come to the "Berghof." After the meal, the Führer
> gives a speech of nearly three hours in which he sets forth his
> political thoughts. Afterward, attempts by individual generals to
> point out to the Führer our lack of preparedness fail pitifully,
> especially the remark by General von Wietersheim, which he at-
> tributes to [his Commanding General] General Adam, that the
> western defenses could be held for three weeks at the most. The
> Führer becomes very angry and blows up with the remark that
> in that case the entire Army was worthless: "I tell you, General,
> the position will be held not three weeks but three years."[29]

Hitler saw the lack of unity among the chiefs of staff at the
Berghof, and he saw also that only one or two of the com-

manding generals had the courage of their convictions. They would be replaced, and the rest would follow orders. He could look with confidence to the meeting with the commanders at the Jüterbog training grounds on 15 August.

The Chief of the General Staff knew what Hitler knew: there was next to no support for his confrontation course, and the senior commanders and their chiefs of staff would carry out orders. Beck made just that point to the Hungarian War Minister during a conference in Berlin on 25 and 26 August.[30] The Hungarian delegation was probably not aware that Beck had resigned on 18 August and that his resignation had been accepted on 21 August, because it was to remain secret for the next few weeks. But on 27 August 1938, Beck handed over his duties to his successor, General Franz Halder.[31]

Beck had gone well beyond making protests and submitting memoranda, not only in his attempts to apply direct pressure to the German government but also in his efforts to instigate pressure from outside. Several emissaries of the high-level Resistance conspiracy now forming itself approached the French and the British governments, warning them that Hitler intended to make war on Czechoslovakia and that he could be stopped only if France and Britain made clear that in this case they would attack Germany. At least one emissary, Ewald von Kleist-Schmenzin, who flew to London on 18 August, was instructed by Beck personally to urge British intervention against the German designs. Beck finally told Kleist: "Bring me certain proof that Britain will fight if Czechoslovakia is attacked, and I will make an end of this regime."[32] Also while still in office, indeed before 15 August, Beck had given instructions for secret contacts through German diplomatic channels to warn the other major powers of Hitler's decision to go to war against Czechoslovakia.[33] Beck continued plotting against war and against the government after his resignation.

General Halder was informed by his predecessor of the planned collective protest and intended "showdown." He was also kept informed by Lieutenant Colonel Oster in Canaris' military intelligence bureau. Halder and Oster knew each other well from the time when Halder had been Chief of Staff of the Sixth Army Corps and Military District VI in Münster, and Oster had been a member of his staff.[34] Hans Bernd Gisevius, a friend of Oster's, was deeply involved in the planning for a coup, and so was Dohnanyi. Witzleben and a number of other officers were in positions to help, as were Hjalmar Schacht, the President of the Reichsbank, and, on the fringes, Goerdeler.

The new Chief of the General Staff insisted that a coup must not lead to civil war and that a stable political authority must be quickly established. But he was willing to preside over the coup and to coordinate it, and he expressed confidence that he could induce the Commander in Chief to tolerate a coup.

Failed Conspiracies 7

General Halder's position was ambiguous. He involved himself deeply in the plot. Under German law, he committed high treason by plotting against the government, and treason against the country by contacting potential enemy governments to warn them of Hitler's intentions. But he had reservations concerning his part in the plot, saying that the integrity and position of the Reich must not be put at risk.

To all intents and purposes, the members of the gathering conspiracy considered Halder the kingpin of the plot. He was in close contact with the Permanent Under-Secretary of State, Ernst Baron von Weizsäcker, mainly through Oster. On Beck's advice, Halder asked Oster what preparations, political and technical, had been made for a coup.[1] Oster could report little beyond the general willingness of key persons to participate. Halder's position was that he would not take an initiative against Hitler until Hitler had given the order to attack Czechoslovakia. This order might be given as little as twenty-four hours before troops were to cross the border. Within those twenty-four hours, Halder was expected to give the signal for the coup.

The conspirators felt a little uncertain of Halder. Oster, Gisevius, and Schacht devised a backup system. General von Witzleben, who commanded the Third Army Corps in Military District III (Berlin), promised to act, if necessary, without Halder's agreement.[2] Units were designated to occupy key points and government buildings. The deployment of the Berlin police was planned in detail: the President of Police, Count von Helldorf, and his Vice President, Fritz-Dietlof Count von der Schulenburg, were both in the plot. Above all, Hitler was to be arrested. There was some dispute in the conspiracy whether Hitler should be put on trial or summarily killed. A plot within the plot was intended to solve this problem. The leaders of the raiding party that was to penetrate the Chancellery and arrest Hitler were prepared to shoot him down on sight.[3]

General Halder had reserved the right to issue the signal for the coup. He would be the first to know if the order for attacking Czechoslovakia was given. The attack would be followed presumably by French and British declarations of war. But Prime Minister Neville Chamberlain's trips to Germany on 15 and 22 September in search of a peaceful solution and the western powers' apparent readiness to grant substantial concessions to Hitler had a confusing effect upon the conspirators. Toward the end of September, France and Britain showed more firmness, and the likelihood increased that Germany would be at war with them if it attacked Czechoslovakia. Hitler, however, was still moving toward war. A general mobilization order was expected in the early afternoon on 28 September, whereupon the conspiracy planned to strike. The raiding commandos were assembled and ready in their quarters. Witzleben's troops were alerted, and the First Light Division under General Erich Hoepner was stationed in Saxony facing the Czech fortifications, ready to cut off the road to Berlin for Hitler's Bodyguard SS Regiment.[4]

But in the afternoon news came of an international conference to be held in Munich on the next day, 29 September. Britain and France agreed to the annexation of the Sudeten region by Germany. At the same time British and French military preparations convinced Hitler to back down. Thus the precondition for a coup failed to materialize. The British Ambassador in Berlin, Sir Nevile Henderson, understood this and wrote on 6 October 1938 to Secretary of State Lord Halifax: "By keeping the peace, we have saved Hitler and his regime."[5]

As far as most people could see, Hitler's aggressive policy had been rewarded by success. Only a few Germans understood that he had backed down before threats of intervention, settled for the Sudetenland, and given up the conquest of Czechoslovakia. German propaganda glossed over rational analysis; euphoria triumphed.

The conspirators had a point in their concern about public opinion in the event of a coup against Hitler. The conspirators might have reflected that what they proposed to do—arrest the head of government and occupy key buldings and facilities—had ended in failure during the Kapp Putsch in 1920 and again during the Kahr-Hitler Putsch in 1923. They might have reflected that Hitler had applied his own doctrine of the "legal" coup d'état successfully in a free society, but that this would be more difficult in a dictatorship. The conspiracy did not in fact have a plan it could look to with confidence, so the coup's chances of success were minimal.

Another effect of Munich was subjective. The conspirators had felt that the western powers were their allies in fighting Hitler and Nazism. They informed them and warned them of Hitler's intentions, urging them to resist his demands. They received no encouragement, no useful reply of any kind, while their supposed allies bargained with Hitler. It was absurd to suggest to the British government that it subordinate its policy toward Germany to the promptings of a group of conspirators in that country. British policy was to make a major concession to Hitler's government. Even if the British government had not questioned the bona fides of the German conspirators, it would have had to leave them in the dark for fear of leaking their policy to Hitler prematurely. The Resistance in Germany evidently failed to understand this fact. They never quite recovered from their disappointment.

Hitler's successes during the next three years continued to demoralize the Resistance. At the same time, the German Resistance, unlike all other anti-Nazi movements in Europe, remained without any Allied encouragement, although a Fifth Column in Germany would have been a welcome aid in the war against Nazi Germany. After the turning of the tide against Germany, in the second half of 1942, the Allies saw even less reason to give the Resistance the assurances it needed and thereby limit the impending Allied victory.

Despite the disappointment of 1938, the conspirators tried again, in the summer of 1939, to mount an effort to avert war and to overthrow the dictator. Emissaries went to England again. Conspirators in the Foreign Office, in Canaris' Military Intelligence, and in the trade union and socialist underground tried to persuade senior military commanders that Hitler must be arrested and tried. The more or less unspoken assumption was that Hitler's bodyguards would put up a struggle during which Hitler would be shot.

An opportunity seemed to arise after the outbreak of war in the autumn of 1939 when Colonel General Kurt Baron von Hammerstein-Equord, Fritsch's predecessor as Commander in Chief of the Army, was appointed to command Army Detachment A in the west. He had several times expressed his intention to arrest Hitler if he ever had troops under his command. Hitler even contemplated a visit to Hammerstein's headquarters. But the visit was called off. A short time later, Hammerstein was relieved of his post. Hitler's visits to the front were confined to Poland through the rest of the autumn. Not until late in December did he finally inspect front-line troops in the west.

Throughout these discouraging setbacks, Carl Goerdeler was the most indefatigably active opponent of Hitler's government. Since resigning as Mayor of Leipzig in 1937 to protest the removal of the Mendelssohn statue, Goerdeler had worked part-time for Robert Bosch, the Stuttgart electrical equipment tycoon, who wanted to finance Goerdeler's underground activities. Goerdeler traveled abroad extensively, warning governments of Hitler's intentions and drafting economic memoranda and plans to settle the issues arising out of the First World War. At the same time, Goerdeler cooperated with other conspirators on ideas for constitutional and social reorganization, forged underground coalitions, and tried to impress on military commanders the necessity to act against Hitler.[6]

In the winter of 1938–1939 Goerdeler drafted a "peace program" which he hoped his friends in America would bring to the attention of persons who conducted western policy.[7] The plan was based on liberal economic and social principles, freedom of the individual under the rule of law, and rejection of Bolshevism, Marxism, Fascism, and Nazism. The proposal asked for international cooperation to curb Hitler. After the occupation of Prague on 15 March 1939, Goerdeler addressed memoranda to highly placed persons in Paris, London, Rome, and Washington, urging world leaders to impose sanctions against Germany and Italy and to issue a call to the German and Italian peoples to overthrow their dictators. A crippling embargo on shipments of raw materials would, he felt, lend force to these proclamations. If the dictators were not overthrown, at least they would be compelled to keep the peace.

Goerdeler believed that the Polish Corridor issue needed to be settled in favor of Germany, that some of the territory Germany had lost to Poland at the end of the First World War ought to be restored, that Germany ought to be given colonial territories and opportunities for settlers in British and French colonies, that Czechoslovakia should be reestablished and neutralized with the Sudetenland permanently annexed by Germany, and that a post-Hitler government should abandon the present bid for hegemony in southeast Europe and cooperate with the western nations everywhere in the world. Such a program, Goerdeler wrote, would go a long way toward eliminating tensions and war and achieving a European federation of states.

Once Britain and France had crossed the threshold from a willingness to meet legitimate grievances to calling a halt to international threats and aggression, Goerdeler's ideas did not carry much weight. But Goerdeler held to them throughout. He never doubted that a settlement of what he considered just claims could guarantee the peace.

Goerdeler's irrepressible optimism, his faith in reason and in his own powers of persuasion, kept him going. In view of his administrative experience and his ability to cooperate with others of different political positions, it was agreed in the conspiracy that he should head the first post-Hitler government as Chancellor. A socialist, Wilhelm Leuschner, was to become Vice-

Chancellor.[8] The Social Democrats declined taking the helm immediately after Hitler's fall. A similar role in 1918 had cost them dearly politically.

After the campaign in Poland, when the furies of war had subsided somewhat, there still seemed to be a chance to contain the conflict. But it would be necessary to prevent Hitler from opening an offensive in the west. Two methods could produce the desired result: western acquiescence in Hitler's newest conquest, or the dictator's demise. The first was not forthcoming. Hitler, in a Reichstag speech on 6 October 1939, offered to keep everything and to let bygones be bygones. Britain and France rejected any arrangement that did not restore both Poland and Czechoslovakia. Prime Minister Chamberlain gave an unequivocal answer in the House of Commons on 12 October.[9]

Once again, the German anti-Hitler conspirators tried to apply the second method, the dictator's demise. Again, hopes were pinned on senior commanders, especially on General Halder and Colonel General von Brauchitsch. It was clear that the western powers would have a military advantage if Germany were off-balance during an internal coup, and it was not clear what sort of peace terms the western powers would find acceptable in dealing with a non-Nazi government. To find this out, Josef Müller, a Resistance emissary who did war duty in Canaris' Abwehr, was sent to Rome. Pope Pius XII agreed to act as intermediary, a contact with the British government was established, and by February 1940 certain minimal points had been settled. Britain would insist on "reparation of the wrongs done to Germany's smaller neighbours," namely restoration of Poland and Czechoslovakia; a decentralized and federal Germany; a plebiscite in Austria to decide whether or not it wished to enter the federation; and "above all . . . security for the future."[10]

From the German point of view, the existence of a non-Nazi government which would soon turn Germany into a democracy again would have been a guarantee of "security" against further aggressions. From the British point of view, this might not be enough. When the British Minister at the Vatican, Sir Francis d'Arcy Osborne, spoke with the Pope on 16 February 1940, he interpreted the term "security" by saying that he "didn't see how we could make peace so long as the German military machine remained intact."[11]

Nevertheless, the German conspirators believed the British reaction to be favorable, and they pressed General Halder to move against Hitler before the order arrived for the attack in the west. Colonel General Beck and Goerdeler beseeched Halder to act. But Halder had had a change of heart. At the beginning of November 1939, Halder had given his reasons against overthrowing Hitler to the Chief of the Wehrmacht Economic and Armaments Office, Major General Georg Thomas: "1. It violates tradition. 2. There is no successor. 3. The young officer corps is not reliable. 4. The mood in the country is not ripe. 5. 'It really cannot be tolerated that Germany is permanently a "people of helots" for England.' 6. Concerning the offensive, Ludendorff, too, in 1918 led an offensive against the advice of everyone, and the historical judgment was not against him. He, Halder, therefore did not fear the later judgment of history either."[12]

Halder believed that the struggle against England was forced on Germany, that there were good chances of success, and that after a victory the Army would be strong enough to impose its will internally. England's peaceful assurances were not credible.[13] On other occasions, Halder thought a coup would be more likely to have popular support after a major German military setback.[14] He showed Brauchitsch the results of the negotiations through the Vatican on 4 April 1940. But this was only five days before the German attack on Denmark and Norway, and Brauchitsch refused to discuss the matter of a coup.

This effectively ended the prospects for a coup. After the victory over France in June 1940 Halder was no more willing than before to lend his hand to the overthrow of Hitler. Brauchitsch had never gone beyond a willingness to "tolerate" a coup. The opposition was reduced to talking and to planning isolated assassination attacks without the backup system necessary for a serious coup d'état. Meanwhile the conspirators tried to create conditions under which the military leaders might consider supporting a coup, by seeking from Germany's enemies the assurance that a post-Hitler, non-Nazi government would get nationally acceptable conditions of peace. Secret contacts with Germany's enemies in the war had to be established for this purpose.

Contacts Abroad 8

Among the conspirators there were those who would have removed the Nazi regime regardless of the consequences. There were also those who wanted a reasonable assurance of what Germany's fate would be after a successful internal revolt. Radicals like Dietrich Bonhoeffer, who did not himself think that assurances should be obtained, were unable to translate their convictions into practice unless they could persuade powerful military commanders to act in the anti-Nazi conspiracy. To do so, they had to be able to argue that Germany would not suffer any loss of territory and sovereignty as a result of a coup. Many conspirators hoped also that the Allies would distinguish between Nazis and Germans who adhered to principles of liberty and justice. This, too, led them to the question of the Allied war aims: Would the Allies make peace on the basis of the status quo ante bellum? Would they insist on restoring the Treaty of Versailles? Would they insist on conditions even less favorable? Would there be losses of territory, imposed foreign government authority and control, or trade and other economic restrictions?

Before the war, the clandestine contacts of the Resistance with foreign governments served the purpose of warning those governments of Hitler's intentions. It was hoped that a firm attitude on the part of the major powers would restrain Hitler and save the peace. As early as June 1937, the Chief of the General Staff of the Army himself, General Beck, on an official visit in Paris, had warned of Hitler's coming military adventures and declared the dictator "pathological."[1] During the Sudeten crisis of 1938, Beck and Undersecretary of State Baron von Weizsäcker were involved in several missions to London and Paris designed to confront Hitler with unbending foreign opponents.[2]

These efforts continued in 1939, although with less conviction. The powers opposing Hitler's foreign policy had given in so often until the occupation of Prague on 15 March 1939 that the Resistance at home tended to despair of finding outside support. An added blow was Hitler's winning the race for a Russian alliance in August 1939 by offering Stalin nearly half of Poland and most of the Baltic States.[3] Approaches and warnings to the French and British governments from Resistance emissaries, such as the lawyer Fabian von Schlabrendorff, Helmuth James Count von Moltke, Goerdeler, the diplomats Erich Kordt, and Adam von Trott zu Solz, lacked a real objective.[4] Britain and France had been standing firm since 15 March 1939. What remained was the fulfillment of their warnings that they would go to war if Germany attacked Poland. After France, Britain, and a number of other powers declared war on Germany in September 1939, this phase of foreign contacts by the Resistance drew to an end. From then on, the principal objective of the contacts had to be the securing of favorable conditions of peace for a government of the Resistance after the internal elimination of Hitler's regime.

One incident, however, did not fall into this wartime category. It was Colonel Oster's solitary campaign to warn Hitler's next intended victims. Oster hoped that their preparedness would give the German armies such a stinging defeat that it would either dislodge Hitler or force him to stop the war. The German attack in the west was planned to strike at France through Belgium and the Netherlands. Every time a date for the attack was set, from mid-October 1939 to May 1940, Oster, Admiral Canaris' right-hand man in the military intelligence service, transmitted the projected date to the Dutch government. He also warned the Danish and Norwegian governments of the impending German invasions in April 1940, six days in advance.

Oster's radical opposition to the Nazi regime had led him to seek Germany's defeat as the only alternative to carnage and destruction.[5] His warnings had no practical effect.

Josef Müller's soundings in the Vatican served the effort to move Generals von Brauchitsch and Halder toward a coup. Through the mediation of Pope Pius XII, these contacts produced a response from the British government and indirectly from the French government. It is not entirely clear what the conspirators were told through Müller or how they used the information. As Halder remembered it, excessively favorable conditions were suggested, which nevertheless did not change the new position he had held since November 1939 of opposing a coup d'état. The terms mentioned in the British diplomatic correspondence bear little resemblance to Halder's recollections. They suggest conditions considerably more severe than those imposed in the Treaty of Versailles: a decentralized and federal Germany, with "security" for the future. Since Versailles had not provided "security" what was required was the division of Germany, the effective control of its military potential, and the prevention of its rearmament.[6] Neither Halder nor Brauchitsch could be persuaded to overthrow Hitler on the strength of the results secured by the contacts when they were informed of those results on 4 April 1940.[7] From then on, Allied governments did not even reply to Resistance overtures, let alone offer encouragement.

As the war became harder, Britain especially appeared resolved not to compromise. In January 1941, Prime Minister Winston Churchill instructed Foreign Secretary Anthony Eden, Lord Halifax's successor, concerning peace feelers from Germany: "Your predecessor was entirely misled in December 1939. Our attitude towards all such inquiries or suggestions should be absolute silence. It may well be that a new peace offensive will open upon us as an alternative to threats of invasion and poison gas." As a result of the German attack on Russia on 22 June 1941, a military alliance was concluded between Britain and the Soviet Union on 12 July, and a month later a cordial alliance, called the Atlantic Charter, was forged with America.

Churchill repeated his position on peace overtures emphatically in September 1941: "I am sure we should not depart from our policy of absolute silence. Nothing would be more disturbing to our friends in the United States or more dangerous with our new ally, Russia, than the suggestion that we were entertaining such ideas. I am absolutely opposed to the slightest contact."[8]

Albrecht Haushofer, a professor of geopolitics and an opponent of Hitler's policies, was well acquainted with Hitler's Deputy Rudolf Hess, and on behalf of the Resistance he exploited Hess's concern to end the conflict between Germany and Britain. Hess enabled him to travel, and during the months from August 1940 to mid-May 1941, under cover and on behalf of the Resistance, Haushofer contacted Wing Commander Lord Lothian, Duke of Hamilton, and Carl Jacob Burckhardt, a Swiss diplomat of international standing and the former League of Nations High Commissioner for Danzig.[9] Ulrich von Hassell also contacted Burckhardt in May 1941 to explain Haushofer's cover and his credentials as a Resistance emissary.[10] On that very same day, 10 May 1941, Hess flew a Messerschmitt 110 to Britain, parachuted down, and let the plane crash. Hess had come to arrange peace on his own. Hitler declared him mad. Haushofer's credibility was ruined.[11] He was murdered by the SS in the last days of the war.

Britain was far from considering any peace overtures. The Anglo-Russian alliance of July 1941 and the Anglo-American entente of August 1941 spelled out the Allied war aims in general terms. Total victory and unconditional surrender, as well as disarmament and "controls" in the future, were written into these Allied agreements and proclamations.

The Allied war aims appeared extreme and unrealistic to the Resistance. They were certainly not a basis on which the Resistance could justify an internal revolt to remove Hitler, unless assurances were obtained that the Allied goals would be modified reasonably for an anti-Nazi government. The foreign contacts of the Resistance from now on were aimed at securing any encouragement from the Allies and some modification of the "unconditional surrender" formula. The German approaches sought various degrees of concession.

Dietrich Bonhoeffer made contacts in Norway, Switzerland, and Sweden in April and May 1942 with church officials who had access to Allied governments, in order to procure enough support to make an internal revolt possible. Since Bonhoeffer believed that Germany must be defeated, occupied, and controlled, it is not clear what sort of reassurances he could have brought home with him for generals wavering about joining the conspiracy.[12] In July 1939, he had written to Reinhold Niebuhr: "Christians in Germany will face the terrible alternative of either willing the defeat of their nation in order that Christian civilization may survive, or willing the victory of their nation and thereby destroying our civilization. I know which of these alternatives I must choose."[13] And during a visit to Geneva in September 1941, Bonhoeffer had told Willem Visser 't Hooft, the Secretary General of the World Council of Churches, "If you want to know, I pray for the defeat of my country, for I think that is the only possibility of paying for all the suffering that my country has caused in the world." He repeated this to his Norwegian contacts in April 1942 and to the Bishop of Chichester in May 1942.[14]

Most of the other emissaries, however, sought to find acceptable Allied terms. Adam von Trott zu Solz, who had worked in the Foreign Office in Berlin since 1940, prepared a memorandum together with several other conspirators which was transmitted to Sir Stafford Cripps, Lord Privy Seal, and to Prime Minister Churchill in April 1942.[15] It emphasized that the German regime could be overthrown in the present strategic situation only by a Soviet victory or by an internal revolt; that it was in the interest of the western world for Germany and Europe to be saved from Hitler's totalitarianism and equally from bolshevization under Stalin; that the Polish and Czech states must be restored on the basis of ethnographic frontiers; that Germany must be made both self-governing and federal and be integrated into a European federation; and that Europe must be reorganized without regard to such concepts as "status quo ante." Trott's renunciation of the status quo was a renunciation of Germany's conquests, at a time when most of Europe was German-dominated and it seemed reasonable to expect that Germany would at least not have to lose territory that had belonged to it before the war. Trott's memorandum also stated the need "to accept our due share of responsibility and guilt." Again, it is not clear how German military commanders might have been persuaded that an Allied agreement with these points could be advantageous to Germany. In 1943 and 1944, during trips to Switzerland and Sweden, Trott continued to plead for encouragement and support for the Resistance, explaining that a post-Hitler government formed by the conspirators would operate on strongly socialist principles, but warning that Russia would "win the game" if Hitler were not overthrown internally.[16] His position was weaker now, and his dilemma more intense. Germany could no longer expect to keep the status quo, even though Trott still had to plead for it, if he hoped to persuade any generals, and perhaps also for his own patriotic reasons.

Moltke, like Bonhoeffer and Trott, accepted the premise that Germany would be and must be defeated.[17] On this basis, Moltke sought contacts with Allied authorities through Turkey during his visits to Istanbul in July and December 1943. In the existing situation, he argued, without a significant western Allied presence on the European continent, an internal German collapse would lead to Germany's occupation by the Red Army. In view of the behavior of both the Red Army, in Poland and the Baltic States, and the German forces in Russia, this was unacceptable. Moltke therefore proposed an internal coup on condition that the western Allies occupied Germany swiftly after the coup.[18] Moltke either knew or assumed the Allies to have an appropriate contingency plan. They did: it was known as the Rankin Plan of September 1943 "for an emergency operation to enter the Continent."

This was a desperate attempt. Moltke had not believed that the military leaders would ever revolt against Hitler. But in September 1943 Lieutenant Colonel Claus Count von Stauffenberg had taken the reins in the military wing of the conspiracy, and now there was hope. Moltke still believed that the unconditional surrender formula should be modified if senior military leaders were to be won over for the coup, but he dropped this point during his second mission to Turkey in December 1943, when he was told by his friends in Istanbul that the Allies would never deviate from their position. Moltke was as unsuccessful as other Resistance emissaries. He was arrested by the Gestapo on 19 January 1944 for having warned someone not in the conspiracy of impending arrest, and he was executed on 23 January 1945 for his Kreisau Circle discussions.[19]

Goerdeler's minimal goal was to maintain the German position politically, militarily, and territorially, as of 1939. His main line of communication with British authorities during the war lay through a friend, the banker Jacob Wallenberg in Stockholm. From time to time Wallenberg had business in Berlin, and Goerdeler was able to visit Stockholm on occasion.[20] Wallenberg told Goerdeler flatly in both April and November 1942 that the way to proceed was to overthrow Hitler first, then to negotiate for terms and, if necessary, to continue the war until negotiations succeeded.

When Goerdeler approached Wallenberg again, in May 1943 in Stockholm, the military situation had deteriorated for Germany. Goerdeler urged Wallenberg to seek a clarification of peace terms in London. Wallenberg agreed to transmit what Goerdeler wrote down in a memorandum.[21] Among the points Goerdeler drafted during the night of 19/20 May were: to install a democratic German government; restore Poland to her boundaries of 1938, with some modification regarding the Polish Corridor; restore Czechoslovakia, presumably to her post-Munich boundaries; negotiate a fair western boundary; disarm Germany, as far as relations with Russia permitted; and give up all Germany's naval armaments and internationalize its Air Force. But German national integrity, Goerdeler argued, must be preserved. Europe's future would be bleak if the German territories in East Prussia and Silesia were ceded to Poland, if the victorious Allies controlled German education, and if the Allies took into their own hands the judicial proceedings against Hitler and his fellow criminals. Goerdeler must have been well informed about some basic Allied war aims because he tried to argue against them.

Goerdeler's position never changed substantially, as shown by records dating from September 1943 and May 1944, before the coup and Goerdeler's arrest, as well as by extensive notes written by Goerdeler in November 1944, when he was in prison.[22] In 1944, both before and after his arrest, Goerdeler insisted on Germany's 1914 eastern frontiers being preserved and on Austria and the Sudetenland remaining with Germany. It is puzzling how a man as experienced and intelligent as Goerdeler could have been so unrealistic. Some allowance should be made for his indulging in overstatement with a view to winning over senior military commanders. But above all, Goerdeler apparently had an indestructible faith in the goodness of human nature and the power of reason.

There were other lines of contact established with the Allies. Hans Bernd Gisevius, an agent of Canaris's intelligence service in the German Consulate in Zurich, contacted Allen Dulles, the European Resident of the American Office of Strategic Services, or intelligence service, in Bern early in 1943. The thrust of Gisevius's approaches was similar to that of Trott's.[23] Otto John, a corporation lawyer with Lufthansa who was cooperating with Canaris' military intelligence, established lines of communication with American diplomats in Madrid.[24] There is no evidence that a serious effort was made to discover if the Soviet Union would treat separately with a post-Hitler government. Trott may have tried once, in June 1944, to meet the Soviet Ambassador in Stockholm; but this story is based on uncertain evidence, and in any case nothing came of the attempt if indeed it was made. In practical terms, all approaches were directed to the western powers.

All approaches, feelers, and contacts produced only one reply: Germany must surrender unconditionally. The German Resistance movement was already handicapped in that it was not fighting a foreign oppressor. Unlike the French, Norwegian, or

Polish resistance fighters, the German ones were not heroes to their people, nor were they martyrs if they were executed. Similarly, the German Resistance movement was the only one among all those against Nazism in Europe that remained without any Allied support or encouragement whatsoever. This situation was exacerbated by the Allied war aims.

Britain's commitment to Poland in 1939 meant that Poland had to be restored to independence. But the Soviet Union was not likely to relinquish without coercion its share of the latest partition of Poland, received in the Hitler-Stalin Pact of August 1939. And Britain needed the Russian alliance. As long as American troops had not landed in France, the Soviet Union had to absorb enough of the German military potential to enable Britain to survive. Poland, therefore, had to be compensated with German territory. Churchill and Stalin recognized the logic of this situation early in the war. Stalin's conception of the settlement of Europe "was drastic and severe upon Germany," as the British Foreign Secretary, Anthony Eden, reported from his conferences with Stalin in Moscow in December 1941.[25]

In July 1942 and October 1943, the British War Cabinet approved the policy of supporting Poland in its claim to Danzig, East Prussia, and Upper Silesia.[26] The British understood and agreed also that Czechoslovakia, once restored, would reannex most of the Sudetenland. They agreed as well that "between 3 million and 6,800,000 [Germans], according to the completeness with which it was considered necessary to effect such transfers," would be expelled from German provinces. These expulsions might help forestall a renewal of German irredentism. The existence of large numbers of Germans outside the German national boundaries had given Hitler leverage. But the measures adopted by the War Cabinet were not likely to succeed unless Germany were placed under long-term foreign controls. Beyond the annexations and the amputations, Prime Minister Churchill, Marshal Stalin, and President Roosevelt favored the partition of Germany.[27]

No German government depending on recognition by the German nation could accept such conditions. But the disarmament of Germany for an indefinite future was an Allied war aim apart from annexations and population expulsions. The settlement after the war should not, as after the First World War, leave Germany free to recover, to rearm, and to reconquer. The Atlantic Charter made this point clear: "Since no future peace can be maintained if land, sea or air armaments continue to be employed by nations which threaten, or may threaten, aggression outside of their frontiers, they [Prime Minister Churchill and President Roosevelt] believe, pending the establishment of a wider and permanent system of general security, that the disarmament of such nations is essential."[28]

Churchill declared in a War Cabinet meeting on 19 August 1941 that Britain's war aim for Germany was to ensure that nation's effective disarmament. The Atlantic Charter received the status of an international treaty by incorporation into the Washington Pact of 1 January 1942. This pact was signed by all governments in the anti-German alliance. In the weeks and months following the proclamation of the Atlantic Charter, there was a considerable amount of discussion in the House of Commons and the press as to its meaning.[29] The intention to destroy German power for a long time to come was confirmed. The British government also made clear that the Soviet Union did not fall under the anathema against "nations which threaten . . . aggression."

The minimal requirements for a national German government were thus incompatible with the Allied war aims. Many of the leading German conspirators knew this. Well-placed persons with access to *The Times,* such as Trott, Moltke, and Hassell, knew it; clear-headed men like Beck knew it; and even the sanguine Goerdeler understood it.[30] They did consider the interests of the enemy powers, but they considered them in the long term, and they gave too little recognition to the Allies' more pressing short-term aim of defeating and neutralizing Germany.

The German Resistance also had little understanding of the Allies' failure to distinguish between Nazis and other Germans. They found it difficult, from their own well-intentioned position, to comprehend that the Allied governments had no reason to have more faith in the unknown quantity of a conspiracy government than in Hitler's. The Resistance's view was clouded by its members' very ability to transcend traditional national loyalties in their struggle against Hitler's menace and to grasp the common interests of all nations in the crusade against barbarism. But they were clutching at straws, and they hoped against hope to persuade German military leaders that an armistice would not amount to unmitigated defeat. Therefore they sought Allied assurances—in vain.

Assassination Attempts   9

Year after year, police authorities in Germany learned of assassination plots against the Reich Chancellor and other persons prominent in the government. In many cases, the alleged assassins belonged to categories of persons who were subject to persecution by the Nazi regime: Communists, Jews, and Catholics. In 1935, for example, a Jewish medical student living in Bern, Felix Frankfurter, wished to attack Hitler, but he could not get near him and shot instead the Swiss Nazi leader Wilhelm Gustloff.[1] In December 1936, a Jewish student called Helmut Hirsch went from Prague to Germany to assassinate a high-ranking Nazi, possibly Hitler; he was arrested by the Gestapo before he could act.

On 9 November 1938, a Swiss Catholic theology student, Maurice Bavaud, attempted to assassinate Hitler in Munich. Bavaud, who had stalked Hitler for weeks intended to use the opportunity of the annual march on 9 November commemorating Hitler's abortive 1923 putsch.[2] Hitler regularly marched at the head of the column, which wound through the streets of Munich along the route of the original march. Bavaud pretended he was a reporter for a Swiss paper and obtained a front-row seat on one of the reviewing stands along the route. He had a loaded pistol in his overcoat pocket. At Hitler's approach, the SA troops who were lined up in front of the stand raised their right arms for the salute. Bavaud could not get a shot off. He hoped to try again later, but he was forced to leave Germany when he ran out of money. He was apprehended by the police with an invalid railway ticket on a westbound train. During interrogation, he revealed his intentions. He was tried, convicted, and executed.

On the same occasion at which Bavaud was unsuccessful, a south German cabinetmaker, Georg Elser, explored opportunities for an assassination attempt of his own on Hitler. Elser was a disaffected laborer with socialist sympathies.[3] On the eve of the commemorative march in Munich, Hitler always spoke to a gathering of party faithfuls in the beer hall, as he had done in 1923. The speech always lasted well over an hour.

In the following year, Elser managed to slip into the beer hall over a series of nights some two months before the commemorative gathering. He installed a powerful explosive device with an accurate timer in a pillar before which Hitler always stood during his speech. On the night of the speech, 8 November 1939, Hitler spoke briefly and left early because, unlike the other occasions, he wanted to be back in Berlin by the next morning. A morning flight from Munich to Berlin could not be guaranteed because of the morning fogs in November, so that Hitler had to catch his personal train. Departure times could not be set on short notice because the run had to be fitted into time slots for maximum speed. After Hitler had left, the explosive device went off as timed and killed several party men. It would almost certainly have killed Hitler had he still been standing at the rostrum. Elser was apprehended as he tried to cross the border into Switzerland. He was shot on Hitler's order at Dachau Concentration Camp in April 1945.

Both the Bavaud and the Elser incidents led to increased security measures. Hitler's bodyguard command had been slow to react. Bavaud was arrested in the same month in which he had made his assassination attempt, but security was still lax in the Bürgerbräu beer hall in October and November 1939. The commemorative march, however, was never held again, partly as a precaution against the possibility of an air raid eliminating the Nazi leadership all at once. Hitler's rare public appearances were protected by vast security operations, particularly when they could be anticipated by the public.

The new security measures helped to frustrate an assassination plot in Berlin in November 1939 by Erich Kordt, a Foreign Office official working immediately under Foreign Minister von Ribbentrop. Also in 1939, the British Military Attaché in Berlin, Colonel Mason-Macfarlane, suggested to his government that Hitler could be shot from a window of the attaché's apartment which looked out on a reviewing stand that Hitler used frequently. But His Majesty's Government took a poor view of this unorthodox proposal.

There were numerous other plans and plots to kill Hitler. The Chief of the General Staff of the Army, General Halder, at least thought about shooting Hitler in the fall of 1939, when the military leaders believed Hitler's plan to attack France could only lead to disaster. During his conferences with Hitler, Halder carried a loaded pistol in his pocket.[4] After Hitler's victory over France in June 1940, one of the dictator's most ruthless enemies, Vice-President of Police in Berlin Fritz-Dietlof Graf von der Schulenburg, prepared an assassination plan for Hitler's victory parade which had been scheduled for 27 July in Paris. But the parade was called off because of the danger of British air raids and larger considerations of policy. There was also a proposal by the Director of Home Operations in the British Air Ministry, D. F. Stevenson, to bomb the parade and kill Hitler. This plan, submitted to the Deputy Chief of Air Staff on 13 July, was abandoned even before cancellation of the parade. Stevenson had changed his mind after considering the probable strength of German air defenses, explaining: "The triumphal march through Paris is in accordance with military custom—we did the same thing ourselves after the battle of Waterloo."[5]

As the war continued, Hitler became ever less accessible. For a successful assassination to take place, a willing and able assassin with access to Hitler was required. Furthermore, the conspirators were convinced that an assassination must be coupled with a thoroughgoing coup d'état. They believed that Hitler's elimination alone would merely transfer power to another Nazi leader, probably Göring or Himmler. A Resistance government would have to take several immediate measures: remove the Nazi Party and SS criminals from government, the judicial system, and other offices at the national, state, and municipal levels; dissolve the concentration camps; release political prisoners; and at the same time keep the military machine intact until an armistice could be negotiated.

Stauffenberg in his General Staff post saw day by day how Hitler committed grave errors in military judgment. Stauffenberg also became outraged when he learned of mass murders behind the lines and in the camps and realized they were ordered by Hitler himself. Stauffenberg and others in the General Staff tried to sabotage criminal orders and neutralize professional errors, with little success. But Stauffenberg was not content "to have tried." He became convinced that Hitler must be eliminated. In September 1942 he declared himself ready to kill Hitler. In a staff meeting at Army High Command one of the officers uttered the well-worn phrase that someone ought to go and tell the Führer the truth about the military situation. Stauffenberg replied: "It is not a question of telling him the truth, but of killing him, and I am prepared to do it."[6] But he had no access to the dictator, and he found no support. He was not even initiated into the existing anti-Hitler conspiracy led by Beck and Goerdeler. In February 1943 he was posted for front duty in Africa.

In the meantime, the wanton sacrifice of the Sixth Army—250,000 men killed—had taken place in Stalingrad in January 1943. From the military point of view, this act was so clearly criminal, and it was so clearly Hitler's exclusive responsibility, that a good number of Army officers were jarred into the realization that Hitler must go. Many of them were willing to act, given an opportunity. Nearly everyone in the German nation understood the catastrophic dimensions of the defeat at Stalingrad.[7]

The specter of Stalingrad drove the White Rose Resistance group of Munich students to precipitate action, the distribution of anti-Hitler leaflets, which led to their arrests and executions in February 1943.[8] Also in February, several officers in the command structure of Army Detachment Lanz in the Kharkov area of Russia resolved that when Hitler made an anticipated visit to Army Group B headquarters at Poltava, they would arrest and shoot him. But Hitler changed his plans and instead visited Fieldmarshal von Manstein's Army Group South headquarters at Saporozhe, on 17 February. Manstein had made clear to Stauffenberg on 26 January that he was not willing to make a move against Hitler.[9]

A few weeks later, on 13 March 1943, Hitler visited the front in Russia again, at Army Group Center headquarters near Smolensk, in order to confer with Fieldmarshal Günther von Kluge. There were about half a dozen conspirators in Kluge's staff, led by his operations officer, Colonel Henning von Tresckow. They plotted to kill Hitler during the visit. Kluge himself was in general agreement with the conspiracy. The conspirators, however, wanted a group of assassins to enter the dining room during lunch and shoot Hitler with submachine guns. The assassins would have to begin shooting as they opened the door, without taking precise aim. Kluge vetoed this plan. He would be sitting next to Hitler and would very likely become a casualty, too.[10]

During lunch, however, Tresckow asked a General Staff officer who traveled on Hitler's personal airplane to deliver a small parcel to another officer in the Army High Command headquarters. Tresckow described the parcel's contents vaguely as some bottles of spirits. But it actually contained two small mines with a thirty-minute delay fuse. The mines would have blown a hole in the fuselage of Hitler's aircraft large enough to cause it to crash. Schlabrendorff, a member of the Army Group's staff who was in the plot, started the fuse before he handed over the parcel at the airfield. But the mines did not explode. Schlabrendorff flew to Hitler's headquarters on the next courier flight to retrieve the parcel, claiming an error. He examined the mines and found that the fuse had functioned, but it had failed to ignite the explosive. Apparently the temperature had been too low during the flight.[11]

On 21 March 1943, a new opportunity to assassinate Hitler presented itself. Another officer in Army Group Center, Colonel Rudolph Baron Christoph von Gersdorff, was scheduled to go to Berlin to take part in the annual Heroes' Memorial observances, at which Hitler regularly spoke before opening an exhibition of captured war matériel. Gersdorff would be in charge of leading Hitler through the exhibition. Ten minutes were usually allowed in the program for the viewing. Tresckow suggested to Gersdorff that he blow himself up with Hitler on that day. Gersdorff agreed. He would carry in his overcoat pockets the two mines that had been left undetonated in the airplane attempt. He received them from Schlabrendorff, with ten-minute delay fuses, on 20 March, the day of his arrival in Berlin. As it turned out, the mines could not be prepared for simultaneous ignition on less than a half-day's notice. Gersdorff therefore had to use the ten-minute delay fuses. He had to start them as soon as Hitler entered the exhibition rooms, keeping close to him until the mines exploded. But Hitler virtually ran through the rooms. Göring officiously tried to point out certain items, but Hitler would not stop. In no more than two minutes, Hitler had left the exhibition rooms. Gersdorff had to stay behind. All he could do was to duck into a privy to defuse the mines.[12]

Germany, and the Gestapo, were in a nervous mood after Stalingrad and after the Scholl Group's rebellion. There was latent unrest, and the Gestapo found grounds for suspicion in many quarters. Fritz-Dietlof Count von der Schulenburg was arrested temporarily on 2 April 1943 on an obscure suspicion of plotting but was released uncharged. The Gestapo also suspected several of the conspirators in Canaris' military intelligence service but could proceed against them only on grounds of financial irregularity. These were connected with the conspirators' underground railroad for some Berlin Jews. The investigation led to the arrest on 5 April 1943 of Dohnanyi, Bonhoeffer, and Müller; Oster was placed under house arrest. When Gisevius was ordered back to Berlin to answer questions, he became uncomfortable during the inquiry, managed to put up a smoke screen,

and escaped back to Switzerland.[13] All this effectively immo-
bilized the Resistance for months.

At that time, from April to June 1943, Stauffenberg was in
the hospital, recovering from wounds received at the front. He
had lost his right hand, two fingers on the left hand, a kneecap,
and an eye, and he had suffered head injuries. When approached
in the hospital in May 1943 by the conspirators, he agreed to
join the plot.[14]

After Stauffenberg's release from the hospital in June, he and
Tresckow put the coup plan on a new footing. Stauffenberg was
posted as Chief of Staff to General Friedrich Olbricht in the
command center of the Home Army, in Berlin. Olbricht was a
member of the conspiracy, and so were several other officers in
this and other military commands in Berlin. The assignment
gave Stauffenberg an extraordinary opportunity. With Tresckow and Major Hans-Ulrich von Oertzen, Stauffenberg re-
viewed and rewrote mobilization orders designed to mobilize
Home Army units in case of internal disorder or an Allied air-
borne attack, so that counteroperations could be mounted under
the codeword "Valkyrie." But the mobilized troops might also
be turned against the government and the party if a suitable
pretext could be created. The plan was to kill Hitler and to
accuse unnamed Nazi Party bigwigs of "stabbing the fighting
front in the back," so that the Army would have to assume
government power in order to "maintain order." All that remained was to find an assassin.[15]

In September, November, and December 1943, the coup seemed
near realization. Volunteers stood ready to kill Hitler. But the
difficulty of bringing a volunteer together with his quarry continued to baffle and frustrate the conspirators.

A captain of the Tank Troops, Axel Baron von dem Bussche,
volunteered to blow himself up with Hitler. He was placed in
charge of a demonstration of new uniforms and infantry equipment to take place before Hitler. Bussche prepared a large explosive charge for ignition with a four-and-one-half second hand-
grenade fuse. On a request from Olbricht's office, sent by Stauffenberg, Olbricht's Chief of Staff, Bussche was given leave from

his post as a battalion commander and went to Hitler's field headquarters to wait. Several conspirators in the General Staff worked to arrange a date for the equipment review by Hitler. But before a date could be set, the equipment was destroyed in Berlin during an air raid. Bussche had to return to his unit in January 1944. He lost a leg in combat and spent months in the hospital.[16]

Others volunteered for the assassination of Hitler. The first of them was Lieutenant Ewald Heinrich von Kleist. After Bussche had been wounded, Kleist offered to carry out Bussche's plan. But the equipment viewing did not materialize until 7 July 1944, and Kleist could not get assigned to it. Major-General Helmuth Stieff, another conspirator, attended the viewing, but he declined to be an assassin. In March 1944, Captain Eberhard von Breitenbuch agreed to kill Hitler but preferred to use his pistol. Breitenbuch accompanied Fieldmarshal Ernst Busch to a conference with Hitler on 11 March, but at the last minute he was barred from entering the conference room.[17]

In July 1944 Stauffenberg made at least three attempts of his own to assassinate Hitler. On 6 July he traveled to Hitler's Berghof retreat for the first time as Chief of Staff of the Commander of the Home Army, carrying with him a quantity of plastic explosive. He apparently still hoped that the tasks of coup leader and assassin could be divided, to improve the chances of success for the combined operation. He must have hoped that Stieff would agree to carry out the assassination on 7 July, on the occasion of the uniform and equipment demonstration at which Stieff would be present. After Stieff's refusal, Stauffenberg had to abandon this plan.[18]

Because of this failure and the other ones in the ten months since Stauffenberg had joined the conspiracy, he came to the conclusion that, if the attack was to be carried out at all, he must become both coup leader and assassin. The date of Stauffenberg's final decision to assassinate Hitler must have been after Stieff's refusal. For Stauffenberg himself to act as assassin, certain factors had to be taken into consideration. First, he was severely handicapped. He was therefore unable to use a pistol in an assassination attack. Tresckow had in any case long since decided that the odds were not good enough for an attack with a pistol. In a crowded conference room, an assassin might not be able to fire a shot before his movement was foiled by Hitler's SS adjutants and bodyguards. If an assassin could shoot at all, he had to aim for Hitler's head and kill him at once. The odds were poor even for a fully competent marksman in the briefing room. A pistol would have to be carried in a trouser pocket, for belts were not worn in the briefing room. The conspirators believed that hidden x-ray equipment might reveal a concealed pistol. Moreover, it was widely believed that Hitler wore a bullet-proof vest.

The second factor of importance to the success of the coup was that Stauffenberg had to survive and return to Berlin. He was indispensable for managing the coup d'état that was to follow the assassination. This meant that he could not blow himself up with Hitler, using a short or simultaneous fuse that would enable him to choose the moment of detonation. He therefore had to use enough explosive to kill everyone in the briefing room, since he could not know where Hitler would be in relation to the bomb when it exploded. Stauffenberg had to use a time-delay fuse. He must activate it in private, deposit his briefcase containing the bomb, ascertain that it had gone off, and escape from the headquarters compound. There was in this method very little that could be assumed with certainty. Headquarters security measures provided for the immediate blocking of all exits in case of an explosion. Anyone trying to leave the inner compound where Hitler's briefings were held had to pass through three checkpoints in succession. These measures were intended for cases of sabotage by construction workers or infiltrators, commando raids, the detonation of mines within the security parameters, or aerial bombing, but the alarm would also certainly be set off by the explosion of Stauffenberg's bomb. In that case the odds against Stauffenberg's escape, which was essential to the success of the plot, were extraordinarily poor.

Stauffenberg was back at the Berghof retreat on 11 July 1944, to report to Hitler on the raising of new combat units to throw into the breach caused by the collapse of the Army Group Center in Russia. This time Stauffenberg did not attempt to assassinate Hitler, because some of the senior conspirators had insisted that the two most powerful men after Hitler, Himmler and Göring, must be killed along with him in order to eliminate any chance for the regime to continue functioning. Neither Himmler nor Göring was present at this meeting, although it had not been unreasonable to expect at least Himmler to be there, because the SS was to train the new units.

Stauffenberg went to Hitler's headquarters again on 15 July. By this time, Hitler had moved his headquarters to Wolfschanze near Rastenburg in East Prussia because of the serious situation at the Russian front.[19] When both Himmler and Göring did not turn up, Stauffenberg wanted to set off the bomb regardless, but found no opportunity to start the fuse. He decided that next time he would proceed whether Himmler and Göring were there or not.

Early in the morning of 20 July 1944 Stauffenberg again flew the more than 300 miles from Berlin to Wolfschanze.[20] He had been summoned to report on the "blocking divisions" that the Home Army was raising to shore up the eastern front. Stauffenberg was to give his report during Hitler's daily situation briefing. Again he brought with him the explosive charge with its delay fuses set.

Because Stauffenberg was indispensable to the success of the coup after the assassination, the plan was for him to leave the briefing room before the explosion. Immediately afterward, the Chief of Signal Troops, General Erich Fellgiebel, who was a co-conspirator, would telephone the news of Hitler's death to Berlin. Upon receiving news of the assassination, General Olbricht, with his new Chief of Staff, Colonel Albrecht Mertz von Quirnheim, and other plotters in Berlin, would immediately set in train a series of moves to seize executive power. The conspirators in the Home Army command would issue prepared orders under the codeword "Valkyrie." Communications between Hitler's headquarters and all territories under German control would be discontinued by Fellgiebel's orders. The coup leaders would use the military teletype system to inform the Armed Forces, and the national radio to inform the public, that "the Führer is dead," that a clique of Nazi Party bosses was trying to stab the fighting front in the back, and that the Army was taking over executive power to maintain order.

Several problems were connected with this plan. General Fritz Fromm, Commander of the Home Army, knew of the plot. He had made no effort to stop it; it was fair to assume he would not challenge the proceedings. But he was not likely to participate unless success was assured. In case of failure, he would probably be on the opposing side. In this case, even if Fromm was prevented from interfering, his neutralization would leave any inquiring military district commanders without confirmation of the Valkyrie orders from their Commander in Chief. They might not carry out the extraordinary orders if they detected confusion and irregularity.

If the attack failed, and if this did not become known for some time, owing to an effective communications blackout, Stauffenberg's presence in Berlin immediately after the assassination attack could have improved the situation. But in the long term the Chief of Staff could replace the Commander only if he could convince subordinate officers that the Commander had been incapacitated through bona-fide causes. If the fact of the failed assassination attack was known at the same time that Stauffenberg sought to initiate operation Valkyrie, the chances of its succeeding were practically nil. The military district commanders would see no reason to obey the orders from the Home Army if they were so obviously based on a false premise, namely Hitler's death at the hands of Nazi plotters. Stauffenberg's absence for two to three hours en route from Wolfschanze to Berlin after the attack therefore added a weakness to the existing ones.

Other factors compounded these difficulties. The Valkyrie orders for the mobilization of the Home Army units were signed by Olbricht and Colonel Mertz von Quirnheim. Upon inquiries from the military districts, Fromm would not confirm the orders unless he had convinced himself the coup was succeeding and unless he had joined it. Stauffenberg could not confirm the orders before his return to Berlin. But if they had not been issued by then and if the communications blackout did not hold, the orders could be countermanded from Hitler's headquarters, whether the Führer had survived or not.

On the morning of 20 July, Stauffenberg and his aide, Lieutenant Werner von Haeften, arrived at the Wolfschanze airfield at approximately 10 A.M. They were taken to the headquarters commandant's commissariat for breakfast. From 11 A.M. onward, Stauffenberg had conferences with officers of Hitler's staff in preparation for the midday briefing at which he was to report. The last preliminary briefing was presided over by Fieldmarshal Keitel in his office hut. The bunker in which Hitler stayed and Hitler's briefing hut were in another small fenced and guarded compound, a little over 1,300 feet west of Keitel's hut. Keitel's briefing ended just as Hitler's was scheduled to begin, and Keitel was always anxious to be on time.

As the officers at Keitel's briefing rose, Stauffenberg said to Keitel's adjutant that he would like to wash up and change his shirt. He was shown into a lounge but emerged again quickly, looking for his aide. Changing a shirt would plausibly explain a one-handed man's need for a few minutes' privacy with his aide. Haeften, meanwhile, who was in a nervous state, had almost betrayed himself. He was holding the explosive while Stauffenberg conferred, but he left it unattended for a few moments in a conspicuous place, whereupon an orderly asked questions about it. Haeften said only that Colonel von Stauffenberg "needed this for the Führer's situation briefing."

Finally the two conspirators joined each other in the lounge. Stauffenberg was to set the fuse on two packages of explosive while Haeften held each package in turn. The two packages contained about two pounds of explosive each, an amount considered sufficient to kill everyone in the briefing room.[21]

In the meantime, Keitel, his adjutant, and several other officers stood outside the front door of Keitel's hut, waiting for Stauffenberg before going to Hitler's briefing hut. Keitel wanted to go, and his adjutant sent a sergeant, the same one who had asked Haeften about the mysterious parcel, to tell Stauffenberg to come along. The sergeant went to the lounge, opened the door, found Stauffenberg and Haeften standing there whispering and manipulating an object, and reported the Fieldmarshal's request for Stauffenberg to hurry. Stauffenberg answered abruptly that he was on his way. At the same moment, Keitel's adjutant called from the front door, "Stauffenberg, do come along!" The sergeant stood at the lounge's door, watching Stauffenberg and Haeften, until Stauffenberg came out with his briefcase in his left hand.

Because Stauffenberg and Haeften had been interrupted in the complicated process of setting the fuses, Stauffenberg went off with only one bomb in his briefcase, or only half the explosive he had at his disposal. The explosives expert in the later investigation, as well as the conspirators themselves, believed that the entire amount, or four pounds, would have killed everyone in the briefing room. This was the conspirators' objective. The sergeant's interruption had prevented Stauffenberg from using all of the explosive. Stauffenberg must have felt that the sergeant would see what he was doing. Stauffenberg's lingering was also annoying Keitel and his adjutant. These factors made Stauffenberg's situation seem awkward and conspicuous. He must have concluded that it was too dangerous to continue the preparations. He may also have had the misconception that he needed to set the fuse in both explosive packages, whereas in reality the speed and heat of the explosion of one charge would have been enough to detonate the other practically simultaneously, thus multiplying the explosive force.

From here on, the course of events was irreversible. When Stauffenberg emerged from Keitel's hut, Keitel had gone ahead, but two other officers were still waiting. One of them, Keitel's adjutant, glowered angrily at Stauffenberg, who returned his black look, and tried to seize Stauffenberg's briefcase in order to carry it for him. The one-armed colonel would not have it, jerking the briefcase out of the adjutant's reach. The adjutant and his orderly later remembered admiring Stauffenberg's energy.

The 1,300 feet between Keitel's hut and Hitler's briefing hut could be covered in about four minutes. While walking toward Hitler's hut, Stauffenberg conversed with the other officer, a general who had also been at Keitel's briefing. The three officers went through the gate of Hitler's inner compound. Inside, the briefing hut was a few paces beyond the guest bunker, where Hitler had been living temporarily since 14 July 1944 while his own larger bunker was under reconstruction for reinforcement with yet another layer of steel and concrete. The midday situation briefings were not normally held in Hitler's bunker, either before or after this date. While Hitler had been residing in his own bunker, up to 20 March 1944, the midday conferences were held in a wooden annex. While he was residing in the guest bunker, after 14 July, they were held in the briefing hut. The briefing hut had masonry walls and steel window-shutters to protect it against shrapnel and shell fragments. These may have suggested a bunker-like reinforcement to Stauffenberg, who had attended a briefing there on 15 July, and he therefore may have expected the explosion to be more powerful as a result of compression. But all five windows were open on this summer day, and there was a hollow space under the floorboards which was noticeable as one walked. The environment thus required a greater explosive charge than a bunker would have needed. Stauffenberg had prepared himself adequately, but the sergeant's intervention had foiled him.

As the three officers reached the briefing hut, Stauffenberg handed his briefcase over to Keitel's adjutant and asked the officer to place him with the briefcase near Hitler so that he might catch what was said before making his own report. He explained that his hearing was impaired from his injuries.

The briefing was in progress when Stauffenberg and the others entered the room. Everyone except Hitler was standing around a heavy, oblong map table; Hitler was sitting on a stool at the center of the table. Lieutenant-General Adolf Heusinger, filling in for the indisposed Chief of the General Staff, was giving a report on the eastern front, while Heusinger's assistant operations officer put maps on the table as needed. There were now twenty-four persons in the room, including the late arrivals. Ordinarily the officer giving a report, who in this case was Heusinger, stood on Hitler's right, while the assistant stood on the reporting officer's right. Keitel's adjutant obliged Stauffenberg by placing him behind and between Heusinger and his assistant, putting the briefcase on the floor in front of Stauffenberg. Hitler acknowledged Stauffenberg's arrival. Heusinger's report continued.

After a minute or so, Stauffenberg mumbled about a telephone call and signaled to Keitel's adjutant. They left the room together. Stauffenberg asked to be connected with General Fellgiebel. The adjutant ordered a sergeant to do it and went back in. Stauffenberg picked up the receiver, put it down, and left the hut. He walked about 800 feet to a bunker where Haeften and Fellgiebel were waiting for him. A car with a driver was waiting, too. After a minute or so, there was a tremendous explosion in the briefing hut. Stauffenberg and Haeften got into the car and ordered the driver to take them to the airfield.

Stauffenberg had little difficulty bluffing his way through the first checkpoint. He growled concerning "Führer's orders" and was waved on. The second checkpoint was equally unproblematical. But at the third, obstacles had been placed in the road, and the noncommissioned officer in charge refused to let anyone pass. Stauffenberg used the telephone, reached an officer in the commandant's staff with whom he had breakfasted in the morning, and got him to order the guard to let him pass. The rest of the narrow cobbled road to the airfield, through a leafy forest, was covered without further delay. At some point en route Haeften threw out of the car the other two-pound package of explosive, which was later recovered. At the air field Stauffenberg boarded a He 111 airplane, provided by General Eduard Wagner, the Quartermaster General, who was also in the plot.

During his flight of around two hours to Berlin, Stauffenberg must have been convinced, judging by his sparse utterances later in the day, that he had killed Hitler. On his way out of Wolfschanze he had passed the briefing hut at a distance of not much more than 100 feet and had gained an impression of tremendous destruction. The air was filled with smoke and debris; uniformed men were running up; cars were moving in the direction of the hut. This was the scene as Stauffenberg and Haeften passed. It looked, in Stauffenberg's words, as if a 15-centimeter shell had hit the hut. No one could have survived.

The bomb went off in the briefing room with a blinding flash and deafening noise at approximately 12:50 P.M. Everyone in the room was thrown to the ground or against a wall. All were burned and bruised. Some were injured severely, cut by flying pieces of wood. Almost everyone's eardrums were pierced. Everyone's hair stood on end from the suction and heat of the explosion. Pockets and boots were full of glass. A stenographer died on the same afternoon; two more participants died on 22 July, and another on 1 October.

Hitler had been leaning on his elbow on the map table when the explosion propelled the table top upward and gave him a tremendous jar. His eardrums were pierced. He had cuts and bruises. His trouser legs hung down in shreds. But apart from slightly impaired hearing and a badly bruised right elbow, Hitler emerged unhurt. After washing and changing, he received Mussolini, whose visit had been scheduled. Hitler showed his awed fellow dictator the ruins of the briefing room. During tea, when it became clear that a coup d'état was being launched in Berlin, Hitler ordered immediate countermeasures.

General Fellgiebel observed more or less the same scene that Stauffenberg had glanced at on his way out of Wolfschanze. Fellgiebel now was to telephone to the conspiracy center in Berlin the result of Stauffenberg's assassination attack. He went over to the inner enclosure, where he saw Hitler walking toward the bunker, singed and with his clothing in shreds, but alive. Fellgiebel went to the communications bunker, a few paces down the path from Hitler's temporary quarters, and telephoned his findings to Berlin. Then he ordered a communications blackout. This measure was designed to protect the conspirators against

any interference from Hitler's headquarters. It happened to co-
incide with Hitler's wishes, but since he had survived and was
still in command, it could not be maintained after he ordered
it lifted two hours later.

Here another flaw emerged in the coup proceedings. If Stauffenberg had reckoned on the possibility of Hitler surviving the
assassination attack, he should have arranged with Fellgiebel to
report Hitler's death back to Berlin regardless. The conspiracy
would have been revealed in any case by the explosion, and the
conspirators could have acted as though Hitler had been killed.
If news of Hitler's survival did not leak out too soon, the coup
d'état could have succeeded on the fiction of Hitler's death.

At this point Stauffenberg either took the position that now
one must act on the assumption that Hitler was dead or believed
that Hitler had in fact been killed. It is not likely that, before
leaving Wolfschanze, he told Fellgiebel that he had used only
half the explosive he had brought. It is likely that he believed
Hitler dead.

When Fellgiebel telephoned the result of the assassination
attempt to his fellow conspirator, General Fritz Thiele, in Berlin,
his choice of words was unfortunate. Fellgiebel said: "Something
fearful has happened. The Führer is alive."[22] He could say no
more over the telephone without compromising Stauffenberg.

The conspirators in Berlin did not know what to make of
this news. The most likely interpretation of Fellgiebel's words
was that the attack had been carried out and had failed. But
there were various possible interpretations. Had the assassination attempt been aborted again? Had it been tried in vain and
not discovered? Or perhaps more plausibly, had Stauffenberg
been caught and stopped before he could act? Had he been
cornered afterward and shot? Had he been killed by his own
explosives, perhaps while setting the fuses, or otherwise through
a premature explosion? Thiele and Olbricht asked themselves
whether or not the conspiracy had been uncovered.

Those questions were reasonable enough. But there was another problem, of which Stauffenberg was aware when he made
his fateful journey. There was among some of the conspirators

in Berlin a lack of ruthlessness which, when combined with the hierarchic military procedures, had created the effect of irresolution on 15 July. This general effect repeated itself on 20 July.

Because of the hierarchical military structure, Stauffenberg, the Colonel, was regarded by higher-ranking conspirators as their executive arm, not their leader. On 15 July, for example, Stauffenberg had been given orders not to detonate his bomb unless at least Himmler were present with Hitler. When Himmler did not turn up, Stauffenberg telephoned his fellow conspirators in Berlin to suggest that he ought to go ahead. Several hours before, Olbricht and others had given out advance orders for Home Army troops around Berlin to mobilize, in anticipation of the assassination. Now they were unable to agree on an immediate answer. Stauffenberg waited, then called again. All of this must have taken fifteen or twenty minutes. Finally Stauffenberg and Colonel Mertz von Quirnheim agreed, without Olbricht's approval, that Stauffenberg was to plant the bomb. By this time the briefing was breaking up, and Stauffenberg found no opportunity to make his move. Olbricht was not only timid but also perhaps too concerned about Himmler's power.

On 20 July, upon receiving the news from Fellgiebel, Generals Olbricht and Thiele decided to take no immediate action. They went to lunch. They returned around 3 P.M., just as Stauffenberg was landing on a Berlin airfield. Haeften telephoned conspiracy headquarters. He said Hitler was dead. Olbricht went over to Fromm's office and asked him to issue the Valkyrie orders. Fromm refused. Olbricht and Mertz von Quirnheim issued the orders themselves. It was now about 4 P.M.

By the time Stauffenberg and Haeften arrived at the Home Army Command center, Fromm had telephoned Keitel and learned of the failure of the attempt on the Führer's life. Fromm suggested to Stauffenberg that he shoot himself. When Stauffenberg refused, Fromm tried unsuccessfully to have him arrested, whereupon the conspirators arrested Fromm.

From this point on, Stauffenberg took over the reins of the coup. But only now, four hours after the assassination attempt, did the teletype orders go out to all military district commands, particularly a general proclamation stating that the Army had taken over executive powers and declaring martial law. This proclamation was signed by Fieldmarshal von Witzleben, who had been ill and out of active service for the past two years. A second general proclamation, providing details for the revolt, was signed "Fromm" and "Stauffenberg." Somewhat later, a short statement over Witzleben's name announced the appointment of General Hoepner as Commander in Chief of the Home Army. Hoepner, a distinguished commander of the Fourth Tank Army, had been dismissed in disgrace in January 1942 for having prepared fall-back positions in Russia for the winter. The inactive status of both Witzleben and Hoepner was of course known. And now Fromm was unavailable for confirmation because the conspirators had placed him under arrest. The unusual orders from Berlin might have raised less question if they had arrived over the names of officials with established authority, or if they could have been confirmed by such officials. But as it happened, they looked distinctly odd and made things awkward for conspiracy headquarters.

The coup orders arrived at their destinations after normal office hours. These orders were not by any stretch of the imagination routine matters. A duty officer could hardly take it upon himself to pass them on; the commanding officer or at least his chief of staff had to be found. Many of these officers were out, away on inspection tour, hunting, or playing cards. As soon as officers with sufficient authority had returned to the military district command centers, they did what soldiers do at such times: they formed as clear a conception of the situation as they could. They called neighboring command centers, and they called Berlin for confirmation. In most district commands no action was taken to comply with the Berlin orders. Worse still, the orders arrived virtually at the moment when the national radio broadcast the failure of an attempt on Hitler's life, at 6:30 P.M. Whatever force the conspirators' orders might have had was now dissipated.

Nevertheless, in several centers the orders were obeyed initially. Troops were set in motion, while here and there Nazi officials were placed under arrest. In Paris the entire Gestapo establishment was arrested, and sandbags for their planned execution by firing squad were stacked up in the courtyard of the École Militaire. In Berlin the government district was occupied for a few hours by the Guard Battalion. Some radio stations were occupied, but the plotters failed to make use of them. An hour or so later, Goebbels convinced the commanding officer of the Guards to accept only orders authorized by Hitler.

By midnight the revolt had collapsed everywhere. In the Home Army Command, General Fromm regained liberty and authority long enough during the night to order four of the leaders shot immediately—Stauffenberg, Haeften, Mertz von Quirnheim, and Olbricht. Within the hour Fromm was himself summoned to Goebbels' Propaganda Ministry and arrested on suspicion of being in the plot. He was tried, convicted of cowardice, and shot on 12 March 1945.[23]

Most of the remaining plotters in the Home Army Command were arrested around midnight. Hundreds of arrests followed as the Gestapo destroyed the German Resistance movement. A "People's Court" tried and convicted about two hundred people who were involved in the 20 July plot. Most of them were executed within two hours of sentencing; appeals were a farce. The condemned men were strangled slowly with thin wire. The first few dozen executions were filmed for Hitler to watch.

Conclusion

The German Resistance attempted to overthrow the immoral Nazi regime and to put an end to crimes of incomprehensible cruelty and magnitude. It succeeded only in demonstrating its existence and its readiness to stand and be counted.

As Hitler concentrated power in his own hands, his removal became the central and most important goal of the Resistance. Numerous attempts to arrest or assassinate him failed. Hitler thanked "Providence" for the narrow escapes of which he became aware. In fact, he was well protected by his security organizations, and his own unpredictability increased the odds in his favor. But security precautions and unpredictability foiled only a few of the efforts by the Resistance. The most promising attacks on Hitler's life, such as those of 13 March 1943 and 20 July 1944, failed after security measures had already been circumvented. They failed not only because of bizarre accidents but for other reasons as well. These reasons illuminate the nature of the Resistance.

Some of the Resistance leaders were disturbed by the contradiction between their purpose to end the Nazi murdering and the necessity to kill in order to achieve their end. They could not satisfy their scruples by comparing the nature and quantity of the killings committed by Hitler and his henchmen to the killing proposed by the Resistance. The Resistance lacked ruthless assassins in its ranks, such as those associated with modern-day terrorism.

Goerdeler consistently objected to assassination. His position was nevertheless contradictory. He never tired of citing religious grounds for his objections to Hitler's assassination, but he kept pressing Stauffenberg to take "action." On 15 July 1944, Goerdeler waited impatiently with Beck for news of the outcome of an "action" whose nature was clear to him, so that he might form the first post-Hitler government and negotiate peace.[1]

Moltke did not believe that the generals would ever make a move against the Führer. He thought it was more productive to stand ready for the day of the regime's collapse than to pursue unpromising plots. He was also troubled by the suggestion that the rule of justice and decency could begin by breaking the commandment "Thou shalt not kill." Moltke gave up his aloof stance when Stauffenberg appeared and did his best to support the coup plan, without, unlike Goerdeler, continuing to object to the assassination.[2]

There were also military officers who hesitated when they could have acted decisively, as on 15 July 1944, when they could not agree on a clear directive for Stauffenberg, and on 20 July 1944, when the news relayed by Fellgiebel from Hitler's headquarters was cryptic. Later on that same day Beck, Olbricht, Hoepner, and Stauffenberg all procrastinated when Gisevius tried to impress on them the need to radicalize the coup by summarily executing some top Nazis. The very outrage at the methods of the Nazi regime became an impediment to a coup d'état, which depended, in part, on those same methods.

Moral principles produced not only an air of ineptitude in matters of violent action but also strength of conviction. The Resistance tried to overthrow Hitler while he was going from success to success. When Beck, the Chief of the General Staff, tried to unseat Hitler in 1938 and was forced to resign, he invoked not only "professional and political knowledge" but also the "dictate of conscience."[3]

The Resistance began trying to overthrow the regime during Hitler's series of successes and victories lasting to the end of 1941; they continued their efforts through his years of defeats. There was no opportunism. All the assassination and coup d'état attempts were made without any assurances from the Allies, so that in any case the defeat, occupation, amputation, and dismemberment of Germany had to be accepted as the result of a lost war. Leading conspirators expressed themselves against Hitler in the most uncompromising terms at the times of his greatest successes. When the war was certainly lost and no power or privileges could be saved, the conspirators acted with the greatest energy and devotion.

Stauffenberg devoted himself to a task that was as good as hopeless. As the effective leader of a coup, he faced enormous difficulties. Success or failure turned on acceptance or rejection of the coup d'état orders by military district leaders and by commanders in and around Berlin. The role of General Fromm, the Commander of the Home Army, was crucial here, but he was not in the plot and might in fact oppose it. As it happened, Stauffenberg, who was severely maimed, was forced to assume the double function of coup d'état leader and assassin. The alternative was to have no uprising at all. Stauffenberg had to act in two places, more than 300 miles apart; in both places action had to be taken at the same time. As the leader of a military action, Stauffenberg found himself carrying out his own orders at the front, as it were. In terms of military rationality and efficiency, the plan had nothing to recommend it.

Stauffenberg's decision to be assassin as well as coup d'état leader had inescapable implications. He had to accept the possibility that he would not survive his assassination attempt long enough to reach the second stage, much less to achieve its ultimate aims. It was likely that he would be killed in the course of the attack. If he survived, his escape from headquarters afterward was quite unlikely.

Since Stauffenberg could not be certain of his return to Berlin to lead the coup, he had to rely on his friends there to carry the revolt forward. After the events of 15 July, he was reasonably certain that he could not rely on them. He knew there was no prospect of substantial support from within or outside Germany. He knew the Allies would not settle for less than unconditional surrender. He knew the fronts could not be stabilized. His brother Berthold Stauffenberg put the position succinctly when he said the worst part was "knowing that we cannot succeed, and yet that we have to do it, for our country and our children."[4] The meaning of the coup d'état was self-sacrifice. Its purpose transcended immediate practical results.

The fundamental ethical motivation was shared to different degrees by most conspirators. There were differences within the Resistance, however, in its military, political, and social concepts for the post-Hitler era. Goerdeler believed in the gradual education of citizens through democratic self-government and in the nationalization of some basic industries. His views were similar in certain respects to those held by Moltke's friends in the Kreisau Circle. The Kreisau members, however, were so adamant that "Weimar" with its political extremism must not recur that they opposed an immediate return to the parliamentary system of political parties; general elections were to be deferred. Even the Social Democrats accepted the need for temporary government by nonelected authorities. In free elections immediately after Hitler's fall, a majority of Nazis might have been elected.

The Resistance was not likely to achieve its aims in any of three areas: securing internal reform, safeguarding an internal uprising through the means of foreign policy, and combining an assassination with a coup d'état. The Resistance acted without any well-founded hope of success. It was not success-oriented in the ordinary sense. But the challenge of total evil demanded a response.

The wars of the twentieth century have been bloodier in quantitative terms than those of earlier eras. In the Second World War, 55 million people lost their lives.[5] Twenty million of them were Russians; of these, more than 6 million were civilians and more than 3 million died as prisoners-of-war. Germany lost 4.2 million soldiers and several hundred thousand civilians in airraids. Two million Germans lost their lives during the expulsion of 16 million Germans from the east German provinces of East Prussia, West Prussia, Pomerania, Silesia, and the Sudeten region. A total of 4.3 million Poles were killed, 4.2 million of them civilians. Yugoslavia lost 1.7 million. Japan lost 1.8

million. China lost 15–20 million. Other nations suffered losses in the hundreds of thousands. Hundreds of thousands of German Communists, Social Democrats, trade union workers, clergymen, Jehovah's Witnesses, conscientious objectors, Gypsies, and ordinary people were murdered in German concentration camps. Over 5 million Jews were murdered by the Nazis and their non-German accomplices.[6]

The murder of the Jews had a special quality. Nothing was more profoundly inhuman than systematic, "racially" motivated extermination. This inhumanity was underlined by its indiscriminate ruthlessness and, in a religious sense, by the fact that the Jews were the Christians' spiritual ancestors. Rational analysis must find all arbitrary killing equally wrong. But the murder of the Jews was wholly extraordinary.

The persecution and murder of Jews was for many conspirators the most important motive to enter into underground opposition. Over twenty of the conspirators arrested after 20 July 1944 testified in Gestapo interrogations that the persecution of Jews was a factor, or the main factor, for their conspiracy. Since the prisoners knew that they could not benefit from open condemnation of the Nazi system, their statements must be accepted as true.

Stauffenberg's brothers Alexander and Berthold cited the treatment of Jews as a motive for conspiracy against Hitler during their interrogation by the Gestapo in July and August 1944. Claus Stauffenberg had expressed outrage and shock on this subject to fellow officers in General Staff Headquarters in Vinnitsa (Ukraine) during the summer of 1942.[7] Peter Count von Yorck during his trial in August 1944 confirmed Stauffenberg's revulsion at the persecution of the Jews.[8] Trott had taken the same position in a 1942 memorandum that was to be transmitted to Allied governments. In the same year Gerstenmaier and Steltzer declared their similar motivation for anti-Hitler conspiracy to the editor of the Stockholm *Svenska Dagbladet,* Ivar Anderson. Colonel Wilhelm Staehle, when responding to his Gestapo interrogators after his arrest in June 1944, accused Hitler of responsibility for the "inhuman treatment of

Jews in the East." Moltke had written to his British friend Lionel Curtis in the spring of 1943: "Even in Germany people do not know what is happening. I believe that at least nine-tenths of the population do not know that we have killed hundreds of thousands of Jews."[9] Moltke himself, well placed though he was in the OKW, did not know the true dimensions of the crime.

Dietrich Bonhoeffer, his brother Klaus Bonhoeffer, Dohnanyi, Leber, Reichwein, Heinrich Count von Lehndorff, Canaris, Yorck, Dr. Rüdiger Schleicher, Mierendorff, Oster, Goerdeler, Colonel Alexis Baron von Roenne, Popitz, and many others cited the persecution of the Jews as a motive for resistance and conspiracy against the government. Major Axel Baron von dem Bussche was the chance witness of a mass shooting of Jews near Dubno in Russia. This event drove him into the anti-Hitler conspiracy. Colonel Baron von Gersdorff, counterintelligence officer in the Army Group Center Command, wrote into the official war diary in December 1941: "In all cases of extended conversations with officers, they asked me about the shootings of Jews without my having brought it up. I have had the impression that the shootings of Jews, of prisoners and also of the [political] commissars was rejected by the officer corps nearly unanimously . . . It must be stated that the facts have become known in their full extent."[10]

Some church leaders—although shamefully few of them—raised their voices against the persecution of Jews. Bonhoeffer's position was uncompromising. He had spoken out against mistreatment of Jews in the church context since the day of Hitler's appointment as Chancellor. The pogrom of 9 November 1938 drove him into political resistance. On 10 November, having learned of the pogrom in his isolated seminary in Finkenwalde, he prayed with his students in the words of Psalm 74: "Thy foes have roared in the midst of thy holy place; they set up their own signs for signs . . . They set thy sanctuary on fire; to the ground they desecrated the dwelling place of thy name . . . they burned all the meeting places of God in the land . . . Arise, O God, plead thy cause!"[11] During the war, Bonhoeffer, Dohnanyi, and Oster organized rescue operations for Jews. These led to their arrests.[12]

The Lutheran Bishop of Württemberg, D. Theophil Wurm, addressed open protests to the state and national governments. He wrote to the Württemberg Ministry of the Interior on 28 January 1943 concerning the "systematic murder of Jews and Poles."[13] On 8 February 1943, he wrote to Württemberg Gauleiter Wilhelm Murr about "measures by which human beings of other nations or races, without due process, merely because of their nationality or race, are put to death." On 14 March 1943, Wurm wrote to the Reich Minister of the Interior of his "conviction that it contravened God's Commandments for humans, without civil or military judicial decision, to be deprived of home, employment, possessions, and life." On 16 July 1943, Wurm wrote to Hitler himself that the separation of families resulting from the persecution of Jews, "just as the other extermination measures taken against non-Aryans, stood in sharpest contradiction to the Commandments of God, and violated the very basis of occidental thought and life: the God-given human right of existence and dignity." Cathedral Provost Bernhard Lichtenberg told his Gestapo interrogators in October 1941 that he wanted to share the fate of the Jews who had been deported to the east.[14]

Hitler recognized more clearly than most people outside the Resistance its true sources. In a military briefing conference on 31 July 1944, Hitler declared that the latest assassination attempt was a symptom of a "moral crisis":

> For this act is not to be seen in isolation, but this act that has occurred here is, I should say, merely a symptom for an internal circulatory disturbance, for an internal blood-poisoning which has befallen here. What do you expect, ultimately, of the supreme leadership at an entire front if, as is now apparent, in the rear the key positions are held by absolute destructionists—not defeatists, but destructionists and traitors . . . For the Russian has not grown that much better, morally, in one or two years—that is not the case—, nor has he better personnel; but without doubt

we have grown worse, morally, because we have had that outfit over there which spread poison constantly through this General Staff organization, the Quartermaster General's organization, the Communications Command and so forth . . . Why is so much being foiled? Why does [the enemy] react to so much in a flash? It is probably not Russian intelligence, but permanent treason which was committed constantly by a cursed small clique. But even if this was not a concrete reality, it would be enough that in some of the most decisive positions there were people who did not continuously radiate force and confidence.[15]

Germany had grown morally worse, according to Hitler, not through its murderous policies but through the internal opposition to them. That "outfit over there" had been a source of opposition to the extermination policy against Jews, Slavs, and commissars. Hitler in effect withdrew the accusation of treason in the same breath in which he uttered it. Hitler understood the moral force confronting him in Germany. He ordered quick trials and immediate hangings for the conspirators: "And most important, they must have no time for speeches!"[16]

The presiding judge of the People's Court, Roland Freisler, consequently allowed no one to explain his motives at length, but a few words did slip into the record. Ulrich Count von Schwerin referred to the Nazi murders in Poland as his first motive, before Freisler shouted him down and called him a common scoundrel. [17] Haeften's brother, Hans-Bernd von Haeften, who was on trial for his life for supporting the conspiracy in the Foreign Office, said at his trial in August 1944 that Hitler was "a great perpetrator of Evil."[18] Yorck said: "The vital point in all this is the totalitarian claim of the state over the citizen to the exclusion of his religious and moral obligation to God."[19] Schwerin, Haeften, and Yorck were all hanged two hours after sentencing.

Some conspirators did go so far as committing treason, although not in the way Hitler suspected. Colonel Oster informed the Dutch government of the projected attack dates in 1939 and 1940. Dietrich Bonhoeffer told Visser 't Hooft in September 1941: "If you want to know, I pray for the defeat of my country, because I believe it is the only way to pay for the suffering my country has caused in the world."[20] Moltke wrote in 1942 to a friend in England, Lionel Curtis, "We hope that you will realize that we are ready to help you win war and peace."[21]

Stauffenberg rejected this kind of radicalism which abandoned nationalism so thoroughly. He condemned those German prisoners-of-war in Soviet camps who supported the Soviet cause and tried to undermine the German military forces, remarking: "What I am doing is treason against the government. But what those are doing is treason against the country."[22] He was nevertheless aware that posterity might not accept his distinctions. A few days before the coup, he said to his wife: "It is now time that something is done. But he who has the courage to do something must do so in the knowledge that he will go down in German history as a traitor. If he does not do it, however, then he will be a traitor to his own conscience."[23]

Selected Bibliography

Notes

Index

Selected Bibliography

Included here are titles published in English. Titles published in German and other languages appear in the notes, as well as in Vera Laska, *Nazism, Resistance, and Holocaust in World War II: A Bibliography* (Metuchen, N.J.; London: Scarecrow Press, 1985), and Ulrich Cartarius, *Bibliographie "Widerstand"* (Munich, New York, London, Paris: K. G. Saur, 1984).

Primary Sources

Astor, David. "The Mission of Adam von Trott," *Manchester Guardian Weekly*, 7 June 1956, p. 7.

———"Why the Revolt against Hitler Was Ignored: On the British Reluctance to Deal with German Anti-Nazis," *Encounter* 32.6 (1969): 3–13.

Beus, J. G. de. *Tomorrow at Dawn!* New York, London: W. W. Norton, 1980.

Bielenberg, Christabel. *The Past Is Myself.* London: Chatto & Windus, 1968.

Boehm, Eric H., ed. *We Survived: The Stories of Fourteen of the Hidden and the Hunted of Nazi Germany.* New Haven: Yale University Press, 1949.

Bonhoeffer, Dietrich. *Letters and Papers from Prison,* enl. ed. London: SMC Press, 1971.

Bonsanquet, Mary. *The Life and Death of Dietrich Bonhoeffer.* London: Hodder and Stoughton, 1968.

Churchill, Winston S. *Blood, Sweat, and Tears: Speeches.* Comp. Randolph S. Churchill. Toronto: McClelland and Stewart, 1941.

Conwell-Evans, T. P. *None So Blind: A Study of the Crisis Years, 1930–1939.* London: Harrison & Sons, 1947.

Dulles, Allen Welsh. *Germany's Underground*. New York: Macmillan, 1947.

Eden, Anthony. *The Memoirs of Anthony Eden, Earl of Avon: The Reckoning*. Boston: Houghton Mifflin, 1965.

Gisevius, Hans Bernd. *To the Bitter End*. London: Jonathan Cape, 1948.

Goebbels, Joseph. *My Part in Germany's Fight*. London: Hurst & Blackett, 1935.

Hassell, Ulrich von. *The von Hassell Diaries, 1938–1944*. London: Hamish Hamilton, 1948.

Herwarth, Hans von. *Against Two Evils*. New York: Rawson, Wade Publishers, 1981.

Hitler, Adolf. *Hitler's Secret Conversations, 1941–1944*. New York: Farrar, Straus, and Young, 1953.

John, Otto. *Twice through the Lines*. London: Macmillan, 1972.

Lochner, Louis P. *What about Germany?* New York, Toronto: Dodd Mead, 1942.

———*Tycoons and Tyrant*. Chicago: Henry Regnery, 1954.

———*Always the Unexpected*. New York: Macmillan, 1956.

Lonsdale Bryans, J. *Blind Victory (Secret Communications, Halifax-Hassell)*. London: Skeffington, 1951.

Martienssen, Anthony. *Hitler and His Admirals*. London: Secker and Warburg, 1948.

Moltke, Count Helmuth James von. *A German of the Resistance: The Last Letters*, 2nd enl. ed. London: Oxford University Press, 1947.

Niemöller, Martin. *The Gestapo Defied: Being the Last Twenty-Eight Sermons*. London: Hodge, 1942.

Noakes, Jeremy, and Geoffrey Pridham, ed. *Documents on Nazism, 1919–1945*. New York: The Viking Press, 1975.

Schacht, Hjalmar. *Account Settled*. London: Weidenfeld and Nicolson, 1949.

Schlabrendorff, Fabian von. *Revolt against Hitler*. London: Eyre and Spottiswoode, 1948.

———*The Secret War against Hitler*. New York, Toronto, London: Pitman, 1965.

Schmidt, Paul. *Hitler's Interpreter*. Melbourne, London, Toronto: William Heinemann, 1951.

Scholl, Inge. *The White Rose*, 2nd ed. Middletown, Conn.: Wesleyan University Press, 1983.

Schuschnigg, Kurt von. *Austrian Requiem*. London: Victor Gollancz, 1947.

Shirer, William L. *Berlin Diary: The Journal of a Foreign Correspondent, 1934–1941.* New York: Alfred A. Knopf, 1941.

Speer, Albert. *Inside the Third Reich.* New York: Macmillan, 1970.

Trial of the Major War Criminals before the International Military Tribunal: Nuremberg, 14 November 1945–1 October 1946. 42 vols. Nürnberg: Secretariat of the Tribunal, 1946–1949.

Vassiltchikov, Marie. *The Berlin Diaries, 1940–1945.* New York: Alfred A. Knopf, 1987.

Wedemeyer, Albert C. *Wedemeyer Reports!* New York: Henry Holt, 1958.

Young, A. P.: *The 'X' Documents,* ed. Sidney Aster. London: André Deutsch, 1974.

Secondary Sources

Abshagen, Karl Heinz. *Canaris.* London: Hutchinson, 1956.

Balfour, Michael, and Julian Frisby. *Helmuth von Moltke: A Leader against Hitler.* London, Basingstoke: Macmillan, 1972.

Bethge, Eberhard. *Dietrich Bonhoeffer.* London: Collins, 1970.

Binion, Rudolph. *Hitler among the Germans.* New York, Oxford, Amsterdam: Elsevier, 1976.

Bracher, Dietrich. *The German Dictatorship.* London: Weidenfeld and Nicolson, 1971.

Bullock, Alan. *Hitler: A Study in Tyranny.* London: Odhams Books, 1964.

Colvin, Ian. *Master Spy: The Incredible Story of Admiral Wilhelm Canaris.* New York: McGraw-Hill, 1951.

Conway, J. S. *The Nazi Persecution of the Churches, 1933–45.* Toronto: The Ryerson Press, 1968.

Craig, Gordon A. *Germany, 1866–1945.* New York: Oxford University Press, 1978.

Dallin, David J. *Soviet Espionage.* New Haven, London: Yale University Press, 1955.

Deutsch, Harold C. *Hitler and His Generals: The Hidden Crisis, January-June 1938.* Minneapolis: University of Minnesota Press, 1974.

Donohoe, James. *Hitler's Conservative Opponents in Bavaria, 1930–1945: A Study of Catholic, Monarchist, and Separatist Anti-Nazi Activities.* Leiden: E. J. Brill, 1961.

Douglas-Hamilton, James. *Motive for a Mission.* London, Basingstoke: Macmillan, 1971.

Fest, Joachim C. *Hitler.* New York: Harcourt Brace Jovanovich, 1974.

Fleming, Gerald. *Hitler and the Final Solution*. Berkeley, Los Angeles, London: University of California Press, 1984.

Friedländer, Saul. *Counterfeit Nazi: The Ambiguity of Good*. London: Weidenfeld and Nicolson, 1969.

Gallin, Mother Mary Alice. *German Resistance to Hitler: Ethical and Religious Factors*. Washington, D.C.: The Catholic University of America Press, 1961.

Gordon, Sarah. *Hitler, Germans, and the "Jewish Question."* Princeton: Princeton University Press, 1984.

Gutteridge, Richard. *Open Thy Mouth for the Dumb! The German Evangelical Church and the Jews, 1879–1950*. Oxford: Basil Blackwell, 1976.

Hamilton, Richard F. *Who Voted for Hitler?* Princeton: Princeton University Press, 1982.

Hilberg, Raul. *The Destruction of the European Jews*, rev. ed. 3 vols. New York: Holmes & Meier, 1985.

Hofer, Walther, ed. *War Premeditated, 1939*. London: Thames and Hudson, 1955.

Hoffmann, Peter. "The Attempt to Assassinate Hitler on March 21, 1943," *Canadian Journal of History/Annales Canadiennes d'Histoire* 2 (1967): 67–83.

———"Maurice Bavaud's Attempt to Assassinate Hitler in 1938," in George L. Mosse, ed. *Police Forces in History*. London: Sage Publications, 1975, pp. 173–204.

———*The History of the German Resistance, 1933–1945*. London: Macdonald and Jane's; Cambridge, MIT Press, 1977.

———*Hitler's Personal Security*. London, Basingstoke: Macmillan; Cambridge, MIT Press, 1979.

———"Peace through Coup d'État: The Foreign Contacts of the German Resistance, 1933–1944," *Central European History* 19(1986): 3–44.

Höhne, Heinz. *The Order of the Death's Head*. London: Secker and Warburg, 1969.

———*Codeword Director*. London: Secker and Warburg, 1971.

———*Canaris*. Garden City, N.Y.: Doubleday, 1979.

Irving, David. *Hitler's War*. London, Sydney, Auckland, Toronto: Hodder and Stoughton, 1977.

———*The Trail of the Fox*. New York: E. P. Dutton, 1977.

Jäckel, Eberhard. *Hitler's Weltanschauung: A Blueprint for Power*. Middletown, Conn.: Wesleyan University Press, 1972.

———*Hitler in History*. Hanover, London: University Press of New England, 1984.

Joffroy, Pierre. *A Spy for God: The Ordeal of Kurt Gerstein.* New York: Harcourt Brace Jovanovich, 1971.

Kernig, C.D., ed. *Marxism, Communism, and Western Society: A Comparative Encyclopedia.* 8 vols. New York: Herder and Herder, 1972–1973.

Keynes, John Maynard. *The Economic Consequences of the Peace.* London: Macmillan, 1920.

Kramarz, Joachim. *Stauffenberg: The Architect of the Famous July 20th Conspiracy to Assassinate Hitler.* New York: Macmillan, 1967.

Krausnick, Helmut, Hans Buchheim, Martin Broszat, and Hans-Adolf Jacobsen. *Anatomy of the SS State.* London: Collins, 1968.

Leber, Annedore. *Conscience in Revolt.* London: Vallentine, Mitchell, 1957.

Leibholz-Bonhoeffer, Sabine. *The Bonhoeffers: Portrait of a Family.* London: Sedgwick & Jackson, 1971.

Malone, Henry O. "Adam von Trott zu Solz: The Road to Conspiracy against Hitler." Ph.D. diss., University of Texas at Austin, 1980.

Mastny, Vojtech. "Stalin and the Prospects of a Separate Peace in World War II," *American Historical Review* 77 (1972): 1365–1388.

Mau, Hermann, and Helmut Krausnick. *German History, 1933–45.* London: Oswald Wolff, 1959.

Mommsen, Hans. "Social Views and Constitutional Plans of the Resistance," in Hermann Graml et al. *The German Resistance to Hitler.* London: Batsford, 1970, pp. 55–147.

Nicosia, Francis R. *The Third Reich and the Palestine Question.* Austin: University of Texas Press, 1985.

O'Neill, Robert J. *The German Army and the Nazi Party, 1933–1939.* London: Cassell, 1966.

Paret, Peter. "An Aftermath of the Plot Against Hitler: The Lehrterstrasse Prison in Berlin, 1944–5," *Bulletin of the Institute of Historical Research* 32 (1959): 88–102.

Peterson, Edward Norman. *Hjalmar Schacht: For and Against Hitler: A Political-Economic Study of Germany, 1923–1945.* Boston: Christopher, 1954.

Portmann, Heinrich. *Cardinal von Galen.* London: Jarrolds, 1957.

Reynolds, Nicholas. *Treason Was No Crime: Ludwig Beck, Chief of the German General Staff.* London: William Kimber, 1976.

Rich, Norman. *Hitler's War Aims.* 2 vols. London: André Deutsch, 1973, 1974.

Ritter, Gerhard. *The German Resistance: Carl Goerdeler's Struggle against Tyranny.* London: George Allen and Unwin, 1958.

Roon, Ger van. *German Resistance to Hitler: Count von Moltke and the Kreisau Circle.* London: Van Nostrand Reinhold, 1971.

Rosenhaft, Eve. *Beating the Fascists? The German Communists and Political Violence, 1929–1933.* Cambridge, London, New York, New Rochelle, Melbourne, Sydney: Cambridge University Press, 1983.

Rothfels, Hans. *The German Opposition to Hitler.* Hinsdale, Ill.: Henry Regnery, 1948.

Scheurig, Bodo. *Free Germany: The National Committee and the League of German Officers.* Middletown, Conn.: Wesleyan University Press, 1969.

Schramm, Wilhelm Ritter von. *Conspiracy among Generals.* London: George Allen and Unwin, 1956.

Snoek, Johan M. *The Grey Book: A Collection of Protests against Anti-Semitism and the Persecution of Jews.* New York: Humanities Press, 1970.

Stolper, Gustaf, Karl Häuser, and Knut Borchardt. *The German Economy, 1870 to the Present.* New York, Chicago, San Francisco, Atlanta: Harcourt, Brace & World, 1967.

Sykes, Christopher. *Troubled Loyalty: A Biography of Adam von Trott zu Solz.* London: Collins, 1968.

Tobias, Fritz. *The Reichstag Fire.* New York: Putnam, 1964.

Trevor-Roper, H. R. *The Last Days of Hitler,* 5th ed. London, Basingstoke: The Macmillan Press, 1978.

Turner, Henry Ashby, Jr. *German Big Business and the Rise of Hitler.* New York, Oxford: Oxford University Press, 1985.

Walsh, Edmund A. *Total Power: A Footnote to History.* Garden City, N.Y.: Doubleday, 1948.

Wark, Wesley K. *The Ultimate Enemy: British Intelligence and Nazi Germany, 1933–1939.* Ithaca, London: Cornell University Press, 1985.

Wheeler-Bennett, John W. *The Nemesis of Power: The German Army in Politics, 1918–1945.* London: Macmillan; New York: St Martin's Press, 1953.

Wilmot, Chester. *The Struggle for Europe.* London: Collins, 1953.

Zayas, Alfred M. de. *Nemesis at Potsdam: The Anglo-Americans and the Expulsion of the Germans: Background, Execution, Consequences.* London, Henley, Boston: Routledge & Kegan Paul, 1977.

Zeller, Eberhard. *The Flame of Freedom: The German Struggle against Hitler.* London: Oswald Wolff, 1967.

Zimmermann, Erich, and Hans-Adolf Jacobsen, comp. *Germans against Hitler: July 20, 1944,* 3rd ed. Bonn: Berto Verlag, 1960.

Notes

Introduction

1. Institut für Demoskopie Allensbach, *Der Widerstand im Dritten Reich* (Allensbach: Institut für Demoskopie Allensbach, 1985).
2. Hans Rothfels, *The German Opposition to Hitler* (Hinsdale, Ill.: Henry Regnery, 1948), pp. 20–21; Joint Chiefs of Staff Directive 1067 of 26 April 1945 to the Commander in Chief of United States Forces of Occupation Regarding the Military Government of Germany, General Lucius D. Clay, in *Foreign Relations of the United States* (hereafter *FRUS*) *1945*, vol. 3 (Washington, D.C.: United States Government Printing Office, 1968), pp. 484–503; Lucius D. Clay, *Decision in Germany* (Garden City, N.Y.: Doubleday, 1950), pp. 7, 10–19; W. Friedmann, *The Allied Military Government of Germany* (London: Stevens & Sons, 1947), pp. 223–225, 261–275, 279; Cordell Hull, *The Memoirs*, vol. 2 (New York: Macmillan, 1948), p. 1603; Earl F. Ziemke, *The U.S. Army in the Occupation of Germany, 1944–1946* (Washington, D.C.: Center of Military History, United States Army, 1975); Harold Zink, *American Military Government in Germany* (New York: Macmillan, 1947), pp. 130–164; Harold Zink, *The United States in Germany, 1944–1955* (Princeton, Toronto, London, and New York: D. Van Nostrand, 1957), pp. 91–95; Gerhard Wettig, *Entmilitarisierung und Wiederbewaffnung in Deutschland, 1943–1955* (Munich: R. Oldenbourg, 1967), pp. 102–106; Justus Fürstenau, *Entnazifizierung: Ein Kapitel deutscher Nachkriegspolitik* (Neuwied and Berlin: Hermann Luchterhand, 1969); Allied Military Government Control Council Law No. 46 (Feb. 25, 1947).
3. Daniil Melnikow, *Der 20. Juli 1944: Legende und Wirklichkeit* (Berlin: Deutscher Verlag der Wissenschaften, 1964); cf. Kurt Finker, *Stauffenberg und der 20. Juli 1944* (Berlin: Union, 1967).
4. Theodor Heuss, "Dank und Bekenntnis," in *Bekenntnis und Verpflichtung: Reden und Aufsätze zur zehnjährigen Wiederkehr des 20. Juli 1944* (Stuttgart: Friedrich Vorwerk, 1954), pp. 9–21.

1. Path to Dictatorship

1. John Maynard Keynes, *The Economic Consequences of the Peace* (London: Macmillan, 1920).

2. Reparations Commission, V. *Report on the Work of the Reparation Commission from 1920 to 1922* (London: Her Majesty's Stationery Office [hereafter HMSO], 1923), pp. 117–146; Denise Artaud, "Die Hintergründe der Ruhrbesetzung 1923: Das Problem der internationalen Schulden," *Vierteljahrshefte für Zeitgeschichte* [hereafter *VfZ*] 27 (1979): 241–259.

3. Gustaf Stolper, Karl Häuser, and Knut Borchardt, *The German Economy, 1870 to the Present* (New York, Chicago, San Francisco, and Atlanta: Harcourt, Brace & World, 1967), p. 83.

4. Herbert Grundmann, *Die Zeit der Weltkriege,* in Bruno Gebhardt, *Handbuch der deutschen Geschichte,* 8th ed., vol. 4, rev. ed. (Stuttgart: Union, 1961), pp. 346–347.

5. Grundmann, pp. 173, 346–347.

6. Grundmann, pp. 167–171.

7. Grundmann, pp. 173–174.

8. Albert Schwarz, "Die Weimarer Republik," in Leo Just, ed., *Handbuch der Deutschen Geschichte,* vol. 4, pt. 1 (Frankfort on the Main: Akademische Verlagsgesellschaft Athenaion, 1973), pp. 191–193.

9. See Richard F. Hamilton, *Who Voted for Hitler?* (Princeton: Princeton University Press, 1982).

10. Henry Ashby Turner, Jr., *German Big Business and the Rise of Hitler* (New York and Oxford: Oxford University Press, 1985).

2. Consolidation of Power

1. *Völkischer Beobachter,* Munich ed., 6 Feb. 1933, p. 1; Thilo Vogelsang, "Neue Dokumente zur Geschichte der Reichswehr," *VfZ* 2 (1954): 434–435; Karl Dietrich Bracher, Wolfgang Sauer, and Gerhard Schulz, *Die nationalsozialistische Machtergreifung: Studien zur Errichtung des totalitären Herrschaftssystems in Deutschland, 1933/34,* 2nd ed. (Cologne, Opladen: Westdeutscher Verlag, 1962), p. 719.

2. Joseph Goebbels, *My Part in Germany's Fight* (London: Hurst & Blackett, 1935), p. 211.

3. *Reichsgesetzblatt, vol. 1, 1933* (hereafter *RGBl. I 1933*) (Berlin: Reichsministerium des Innern, 1933), pp. 35–41.

4. *RGBl. I 1933,* p. 43.

5. Berthold Spuler, *Regenten und Regierungen der Welt: Minister-Ploetz,* pt. 2, vol. 4, 2nd ed. (Würzburg: A. G. Ploetz Verlag, 1964), p. 478.

6. Goebbels, p. 215.

7. *Völkischer Beobachter,* Munich ed., 21 Feb. 1933, p. 1.

8. Herbert Michaelis and Ernst Schraepler, ed., *Ursachen und Folgen: Vom deutschen Zusammenbruch 1918 und 1945 bis zur staatlichen Neuordnung Deutschlands in der Gegenwart,* vol. 9 (Berlin: Dokumenten-Verlag Dr. Herbert Wendler, n.d.), pp. 38–40.

9. *Trial of the Major War Criminals before the International Military Tribunal: Nuremberg 14 November 1945–1 October 1946,* vol. 35 (Nuremberg: Secretariat of the Tribunal, 1949), nos. 203D-204D, pp. 42–48.

10. Karlheinz Niclauss, *Die Sowjetunion und Hitlers Machtergreifung: Eine Studie über die deutsch-russischen Beziehungen der Jahre 1929 bis 1935* (Bonn: Röhrscheid, 1966); Thomas Weingartner, *Stalin und der Aufstieg Hitlers: Die Deutschlandpolitik der Sowjetunion und der Kommunistischen Internationale, 1929–1934* (Berlin: de Gruyter, 1970); Hermann Weber, *Hauptfeind Sozialdemokratie: Strategie und Taktik der KPD, 1929–1933* (Düsseldorf: Droste, 1982); C. D. Kernig, ed., *Marxism, Communism, and Western Society: A Comparative Encyclopedia,* vol. 2 (New York: Herder and Herder, 1972), pp. 70–99.

11. See Fritz Tobias, *The Reichstag Fire* (New York: Putnam, 1964); Uwe Backes, Karl-Heinz Janssen, Eckhard Jesse, Henning Köhler, Hans Mommsen, and Fritz Tobias, *Reichstagsbrand—Aufklärung einer historischen Legende* (Munich and Zurich: Piper, 1986).

12. *RGBl. I 1933,* p. 83.

13. Walther Hofer, "Die Diktatur Hitlers bis zum Beginn des Zweiten Weltkrieges," in Leo Just, ed., *Handbuch der Deutschen Geschichte,* vol. 4, pt. 2 (Constance: Akademische Verlagsgesellschaft Athenaion Dr. Albert Hachfeld, 1965), pp. 17–18.

14. Grundmann, pp. 346–347.

15. *RGBl. I 1933,* pp. 85–87.

16. *RGBl. I 1933,* p. 135.

17. *RGBl. I 1933,* p. 136.

18. Konrad Repgen, "Ein KPD-Verbot im Jahre 1933?" *Historische Zeitschrift* (hereafter HZ) 240 (1985): 67–98.

19. Hofer, p. 20.

20. *RGBl. I 1933,* p. 141.

21. *RGBl. I 1937* (Berlin: Reichsverlagsamt, 1937), p. 105; *RGBl. I 1939* (Berlin: Reichsverlagsamt, 1939), p. 95; *RGBl. I 1943* (Berlin: Reichsverlagsamt, 1943), p. 295; Hofer, p. 21.

22. *RGBl. I 1933,* pp. 153, 173.

23. Repgen, pp. 86–94.

24. Hofer, p. 23; *Völkischer Beobachter,* Munich ed., 23 June 1933, p. 1.

25. *RGBl. I 1933,* p. 479.

26. *RGBl. I 1933,* p. 1016; Hofer, p. 25.

27. Cf. Ernst Röhm, *Die Geschichte eines Hochverräters* (Munich: Franz Eher Nachfolger, 1928).

28. See Hermann Mau, "Die 'Zweite Revolution'—der 30. Juni 1934," VfZ 1 (1953): 119–137; Hofer, pp. 25–36; Klaus-Jürgen Müller, *Das Heer und Hitler: Armee und nationalsozialistisches Regime, 1933–1940* (Stuttgart: Deutsche Verlags-Anstalt, 1969), pp. 88–141; Heinz Höhne, *Mordsache Röhm: Hitlers Durchbruch zur Alleinherrschaft, 1933–1934* (Reinbeck bei Hamburg: Rowohlt Taschenbuch, 1984).

29. General Curt Liebmann, Niederschriften von Besprechungen mit den Befehlshabern usw. des Heeres vor und nach 1933 (here: statements by Chef des Ministeramts im Reichswehrministerium, 25 Oct. 1930), Institut für Zeitgeschichte, Munich (hereafter IfZ), ED I/1–2; see also Hitler's assessment of military worth of the SA, 27 Feb. 1934, as "equal to zero" in Besprechung des Chef HL (Fritsch) und Hitlerrede am 27.2.1934, IfZ, ED I/1–2.

30. Göring was Ministerpresident of Prussia from 11 April 1933 to 24 April 1945. He turned over the position of Prussian Minister of the Interior to Frick on 1 May 1934. Spuler, p. 478. In 1933–1934 Himmler gradually took charge of all political-police forces in the states, except in Prussia and Schaumburg-Lippe. In Prussia he became Deputy Gestapo Chief and Inspector General on 20 April 1934, when the SA crisis was looming. Heydrich became Himmler's deputy and Chief of the Prussian Gestapo Bureau. Himmler was put in charge of all German police forces on 17 June 1936 when the office of Chief of German Police was combined institutionally with the party office of SS Reich Leader. Peter Hoffmann, *Hitler's Personal Security* (Cambridge: MIT Press, 1979), pp. 30–31.

31. *Der Prozess gegen die Hauptkriegsverbrecher vor dem Internationalen Militärgerichtshof Nürnberg, 14. November 1945–1. Oktober 1946*, vol. 16 (Nürnberg: Secretariat of the Tribunal, 1948), pp. 326–328; Höhne, pp. 275–278; *Trial*, XXXV, 391–393; *Documents on German Foreign Policy, 1918–1945: From the Archives of the German Foreign Ministry*, ser. C (hereafter *DGFP* C), vol. 3 (London: HMSO, 1959), no. 123, pp. 252–253.

32. *RGBl. I 1934* (Berlin: Reichsverlagsamt, 1934), p. 529; *Völkischer Beobachter*, North German ed., 15–16 July 1934, pp. 1–2 and supp.

33. Müller, *Heer*, pp. 125–127.

34. *RGBl. I 1934*, p. 747.

35. Müller, *Heer*, p. 135. The oath formula was not put into law until 20 August 1934. *RGBl. I, 1934*, p. 785.

3. Toward World Conquest

1. *DGFP* C, vol. 5 (1966), no. 490, pp. 853–862.
2. Stolper, pp. 132–157.

3. *RGBl. II 1933,* pp. 679-690; *Völkischer Beobachter,* North German ed., 11 July 1933, p. 2.

4. *DGFP* C, vol. 1 (1957), pp. 669–678.

5. Hofer, p. 39.

6. Helmuth K. G. Rönnefarth and Heinrich Euler, *Konferenzen und Verträge: Vertrags-Ploetz,* pt. 2, vol. 4, rev. ed. (Würzburg: A. G. Ploetz, 1959), pp. 130–132; "Traité d'assistance mutuelle entre la France et l'Union des Républiques Soviétiques Socialistes: Signé à Paris, le 2 Mai 1935," in *League of Nations Treaty Series,* vol. 167 (Geneva: League of Nations Secretariat, 1936), no. 3881, pp. 396–402, 404–406.

7. *Treaty of Peace between the Allied and Associated Powers and Germany Signed at Versailles, June 28th, 1919* (London: HMSO, 1919), art. 49 and annex, also in British Parliament Sessional Papers, 1919, Cmd. 153.

8. Hofer, p. 45.

9. Hofer, p. 47; *Note Delivered by His Majesty's Ambassador in Berlin to the German Government on March 18, 1935* (London: HMSO, 1935), also in *Accounts and Papers: Fourteen Volumes. (13.) State Papers. Session 20 November 1934–25 October 1935,* vol. 24 (London: HMSO, 1935), Cmd. 4848; cf. *Documents on British Foreign Policy, 1919–1939* (hereafter *DBFP*), 2nd ser., vol. 12 (London: HMSO, 1972), no. 591, p. 659.

10. *Exchange of Notes between His Majesty's Government in the United Kingdom and the German Government regarding the Limitation of Naval Armaments, London, June 18, 1935* (London: HMSO, 1935), also in *Accounts and Papers,* 1935, vol. 24, Cmd. 4930, 4953; *DBFP,* 2nd ser., vol. 13 (1973), pp. 413–418, 426–432; Hofer, pp. 49–50.

11. Hofer, p. 52.

12. Max Domarus, *Hitler: Reden und Proklamationen, 1932–1945* (Neustadt a. d. Aisch: Verlagsdruckerei Schmidt, 1962), p. 759 and passim.

13. *DGFP* D, vol. 1 (1949), no. 19, pp. 29–39.

14. *Trial,* vol. 20 (1948), p. 624.

15. See Harold C. Deutsch, *Hitler and His Generals: The Hidden Crisis, January–June 1938* (Minneapolis: University of Minnesota Press, 1974); Peter Hoffmann, review in *Militärgeschichtliche Mitteilungen,* no. 2 (1976): 196–201.

16. *RGBl. I 1938,* p. 111.

17. *Trial,* vol. 31 (1948), pp. 366–369; Hofer, pp. 135–139.

18. Karl Dietrich Erdmann, *Die Zeit der Weltkriege,* in Bruno Gebhardt, *Handbuch der deutschen Geschichte,* 9th ed. (Stuttgart: Ernst Klett, 1976), IV, 478–479; Hofer, pp. 139–147.

19. *DGFP* C, V, 861.

20. Hildegard von Kotze and Helmut Krausnick, ed., *"Es spricht der Führer": 7 exemplarische Hitler-Reden* (Gütersloh: Sigbert Mohn Verlag, 1966),

pp. 147–148; cf. Rudolph Binion, *Hitler among the Germans* (New York, Oxford, and Amsterdam: Elsevier, 1976, pp. 26–34.

21. See *RGBl. I 1933*, pp. 480, 538; Raul Hilberg, *The Destruction of the European Jews*, rev. ed. (New York: Holmes & Meier, 1985), I, 34–47; Wolfgang Scheffler, *Judenverfolgung im Dritten Reich*, rev. ed. (Berlin: Colloquium, 1964), pp. 27–32; Uwe Dietrich Adam, *Judenpolitik im Dritten Reich* (Düsseldorf: Droste, 1972), pp. 204–216; "Urkunden zur Judenpolitik des Dritten Reiches: Dokumente zur Reichskristallnacht," *Aus Politik und Zeitgeschichte: Beilage zur Wochenzeitung "Das Parlament"* 45(1954): 581–596; 46(1954): 601–607; Helmut Heiber, "Der Fall Grünspan," *VfZ* 5 (1957): 134–172.

22. Cf. Binion; Eberhard Jäckel and Jürgen Rohwer, ed., *Der Mord an den Juden im Zweiten Weltkrieg: Entschlussbildung und Verwirklichung* (Stuttgart: Deutsche Verlags-Anstalt, 1985); Gerald Fleming, *Hitler and the Final Solution* (Berkeley, Los Angeles, and London: University of California Press, 1984).

23. Binion, pp. 26–34; Paul Sauer, *Württemberg in der Zeit des Nationalsozialismus* (Ulm: Süddeutsche Verlagsgesellschaft, 1975), pp. 405–411, 416.

24. Alfred-Ingemar Berndt, *Der Marsch ins Grossdeutsche Reich*, 4th ed. (Munich: Eher, 1940), p. 222; Paul Schmidt, *Hitler's Interpreter* (Melbourne, London, and Toronto: William Heineman, 1951), p. 105.

25. William L. Shirer, *Berlin Diary: The Journal of a Foreign Correspondent, 1934–1941* (New York: Alfred A. Knopf, 1941), pp. 142–143.

26. Wilhelm Treue, "Rede Hitlers vor der deutschen Presse (10. November 1938)," *VfZ* 6 (1958): 175–191.

27. Hofer, pp. 147–157.

28. *Trial*, vol. 37 (1949), pp. 546–556.

29. *DGFP* D, vol. 7 (1956), nos. 228–229, pp. 245–247.

30. See Herbert Michaelis, "Der Zweite Weltkrieg, 1939–1945," in Just, *Handbuch der Deutschen Geschichte*, vol. 4, pt. 2 (Constance: Akademische Verlagsgesellschaft Athenaion Dr. Albert Hachfeld, 1965), pp. 3–356; Erdmann, pp. 498–591.

31. *The Times*, Royal ed., 4 Sept. 1939, p. 8; 7 Sept. 1939, p. 6; 11 Sept. 1939, p. 8.

32. See *Akten zur deutschen auswärtigen Politik, 1918–1945*, ser. D, *1937–1945* (hereafter *ADAP* D), vol. 11, pt. 1 (Bonn: Gebr. Hermes, 1964), nos. 325–329, pp. 448–478; *DGFP* D, vol. 11 (1961), pp. 533–570.

33. Jäckel and Rohwer.

34. *DBFP*, 3rd ser., vol. 7 (1954), no. 314, pp. 257–259.

35. See Hilberg, vol. 2, ch. 7; vol. 3, chs. 8–9; and app. B; Jäckel and Rohwer; Helmut Krausnick and Heinrich Wilhelm, *Die Truppe des Weltanschauungskrieges: Die Einsatzgruppen der Sicherheitspolizei und des SD, 1938–1942* (Stuttgart: Deutsche Verlags-Anstalt, 1981); Ino Arndt and Wolfgang

Scheffler, "Organisierter Massenmord an Juden in nationalsozialistischen Vernichtungslagern: Ein Beitrag zur Richtigstellung apologetischer Literatur," *VfZ* 24 (1976): 105–135; Alfred Cattani, "Dokumentation eines Kriegsverbrecherprozesses," *Neue Zürcher Zeitung*, Long-distance ed., no. 284, 6 Dec. 1984, p. 9.

36. Eberhard Jäckel, "Die deutsche Kriegserklärung an die Vereinigten Staaten von 1941," in *Im Dienste Deutschlands und des Rechtes: Festschrift für Wilhelm G. Grewe* (Baden-Baden: Nomos Verlagsgesellschaft, 1981), pp. 117–137; Michaelis, pp. 212–216; Samuel Eliot Morison, *The Two-Ocean War: A Short History of the United States Navy in the Second World War* (Boston and Toronto: Little, Brown, 1963).

37. Statistisches Bundesamt, ed., *Statistisches Jahrbuch für die Bundesrepublik Deutschland: 1960* (Stuttgart and Mainz: W. Kohlhammer, 1960), pp. 78–79.

38. *Kriegstagebuch des Oberkommandos der Wehrmacht (Wehrmachtführungsstab)*, vol. 4, ed. Percy Ernst Schramm (Frankfort on the Main: Bernard & Graefe Verlag für Wehrwesen, 1961), pp. 55–56, 1712, 1721.

39. Cf. Binion.

4. Forces of Opposition

1. Berndt, p. 222; Schmidt, p. 105; Shirer, pp. 142–143; Sarah Gordon, *Hitler, Germans, and the "Jewish Question"* (Princeton: Princeton University Press, 1984); Treue, pp. 175–191.

2. Inge Scholl, *The White Rose*, 2nd ed. (Middletown, Conn.: Wesleyan University Press, 1983), pp. 89–90.

3. Miles [Walter Löwenheim], *Neu beginnen! Faschismus oder Sozialismus: Als Diskussionsgrundlage der Sozialisten Deutschlands* (Karlsbad: Graphia, 1933); Kurt Kliem, "Der sozialistische Widerstand gegen das dritte Reich dargestellt an der Gruppe 'Neu Beginnen,'" Ph.D. diss., University of Marburg, 1957; Hans J. Reichhardt, "Neu Beginnen: Ein Beitrag zur Geschichte des Widerstandes der Arbeiterbewegung gegen den Nationalsozialismus," in *Jahrbuch für die Geschichte Mittel-und Ostdeutschlands* 12 (1963): 150–188; cf. Weber.

4. Günther Weisenborn, *Der lautlose Aufstand: Bericht über die Widerstandsbewegung des deutschen Volkes 1933–1945* (Hamburg: Rowohlt, 1962), pp. 30–32; Detlev Peukert, *Die KPD im Widerstand: Verfolgung und Untergrundarbeit an Rhein und Ruhr, 1933 bis 1945* (Wuppertal: Peter Hammer, 1980); Detlev Peukert, *Volksgenossen und Gemeinschaftsfremde: Anpassung, Ausmerze und Aufbegehren unter dem Nationalsozialismus* (Cologne: Bund-Verlag, 1982); Detlev J. K. Peukert, "Volksfront und Volksbewegungskonzept im kommunistischen Widerstand: Thesen," in Jürgen Schmädeke and Peter Steinbach, *Der Widerstand gegen den Nationalsozialismus: Die deutsche Gesellschaft und der Widerstand gegen Hitler* (Munich and Zurich: Piper, 1985),

pp. 875–887; Ian Kershaw, *Popular Opinion and Political Dissent in the Third Reich: Bavaria, 1933–1945* (Oxford: Clarendon Press, 1983); Ian Kershaw, " 'Widerstand ohne Volk?' Dissens und Widerstand im Dritten Reich," in Schmädeke and Steinbach, pp. 779–798; Ian Kershaw, *Der Hitler-Mythos: Volksmeinung und Propaganda im Dritten Reich* (Stuttgart: Deutsche Verlags-Anstalt, 1980); Otto Dov Kulka, " 'Public Opinion' in Nazi Germany and the 'Jewish Question,' " *The Jerusalem Quarterly*, no. 25 (1982): 121–144; Otto Dov Kulka, " 'Public Opinion' in Nazi Germany: The Final Solution," *The Jerusalem Quarterly*, no. 26 (1983): 34–45.

5. Rudolf Pechel, *Deutscher Widerstand* (Erlenbach and Zurich: Eugen Rentsch, 1947), pp. 80–81.

6. Pechel, *Widerstand*, pp. 82–84; Rudolf Pechel, "Tatsachen," *Deutsche Rundschau* 69 (1946): 173–180; Harald Poelchau, *Die letzten Stunden: Erinnerungen eines Gefängnispfarrers aufgezeichnet von Graf Alexander Stenbock-Fermor* (Berlin: Verlag Volk und Welt, 1949), pp. 96–99; Indictment of Chief Reich Prosecutor, People's Court, of 15 Feb. 1944 against Robert Uhrig, Walter Budeus, Kurt Lehmann, Willy Sachse, Fritz Riedel, Karl Frank, Leopold Tomschik, Franz Mett, Rudolf Grieb, Erich Kurz, Paul Gesche, and Otto Klippenstein, Berlin Document Center (hereafter BDC).

7. People's Court case against R. Mewes 1943, BDC; David J. Dallin, *Soviet Espionage* (New Haven and London: Yale University Press, 1955), pp. 234–262; Peter Hoffmann, *The History of the German Resistance, 1933–1945* (London: Macdonald and Jane's; Cambridge: MIT Press, 1977), pp. 23–33; W. F. Flicke, *Spionagegruppe Rote Kapelle* (Wels: Verlag Welsermühl, 1957); Heinz Höhne, *Codeword Director* (London: Secker and Warburg, 1971).

8. Walter Wagner, *Der Volksgerichtshof im nationalsozialistischen Staat* (Stuttgart: Deutsche Verlags-Anstalt, 1974), pp. 277–415.

9. Fabian von Schlabrendorff, *The Secret War against Hitler* (New York, Toronto, and London: Pitman, 1965), pp. 44–45.

10. Eberhard Bethge, *Dietrich Bonhoeffer* (London: Collins, 1970), pp. 649–654.

11. Hoffmann, *History*, pp. 30–31; Wagner, pp. 262–276.

12. See J. G. de Beus, *Tomorrow at Dawn!* (New York and London: W. W. Norton, 1980); Hermann Graml, "Der Fall Oster," *VfZ* 14 (1966): 26–39; Romedio Galeazzo Graf von Thun-Hohenstein, *Der Verschwörer: General Oster und die Militäropposition* (Berlin: Severin und Siedler, 1982); Hoffmann, *History*, pp. 140, 169–172.

13. Eberhard Bethge, "Dietrich Bonhoeffer und die Juden," in Ernst Feil and Ilse Tödt, ed., *Konsequenzen: Dietrich Bonhoeffers Kirchenverständnis heute* (Munich: Chr. Kaiser, 1980), pp. 171–214.

14. Heinz Boberach, *Meldungen aus dem Reich* (Neuwied: Hermann Luchterhand, 1965); Jeremy Noakes and Geoffrey Pridham, ed., *Documents on Nazism, 1919–1945* (New York: The Viking Press, 1975), pp. 296–327,

654–669; Adolf Hitler, *Hitler's Secret Conversations, 1941–1944* (New York: Farrar, Straus, and Young, 1953), pp. 117, 316, 332, 366–368, 447–451.

15. Alexander Mitscherlich and Fred Mielke, ed., *Medizin ohne Menschlichkeit: Dokumente des Nürnberger Ärzteprozesses* (Frankfort on the Main: Fischer Taschenbuch, 1979), pp. 183–230; Arndt, Scheffler; Eugen Kogon et al., ed., *Nationalsozialistische Massentötungen durch Giftgas: Eine Dokumentation* (Frankfort on the Main; S. Fischer, 1983), pp. 27–80.

16. Gerhard Schäfer, ed., *Landesbischof D. Wurm und der nationalsozialistische Staat, 1940–1945* (Stuttgart: Calwer, 1968), pp. 113–146; Heinrich Portmann, *Cardinal von Galen* (London: Jarrolds, 1957), pp. 99–113; J. S. Conway, *The Nazi Persecution of the Churches, 1933–45* (Toronto: The Ryerson Press, 1968), pp. 269–272, 280–281.

17. Hitler, *Conversations*, pp. 117, 332, 447–451; Henry Picker, *Hitlers Tischgespräche im Führerhauptquartier, 1941–1942*, 2nd ed. (Stuttgart: Seewald, 1965), pp. 176–178, 436–439; Albert Speer, *Inside the Third Reich* (New York: Macmillan, 1970), p. 123. ،

18. See Lawrence D. Stokes, "The German People and the Destruction of the European Jews," *Central European History* 6 (1973): 167–191; Gordon.

19. Gordon; Stokes, pp. 173–175.

20. Gordon, pp. 214–215.

21. Gordon, pp. 300–308.

22. Hitler, *Conversations*, pp. 316, 367–368, 519; Georg Ruppelt, "Die 'Ausschaltung' des 'Wilhelm Tell,' " *Jahrbuch der Deutschen Schillergesellschaft* 20 (1976): 402–419.

23. Speer, p. 158.

5. Varieties of Thought

1. Kernig, pp. 70–89.

2. See Franz Josef Furtwängler, *Männer, die ich sah und kannte* (Hamburg: Auerdruck, 1951), pp. 215–216; Otto John, "Männer im Kampf gegen Hitler (IV): Wilhelm Leuschner," *Blick in die Welt* 2.9 (1947): 20; Julius Leber, *Ein Mann geht seinen Weg: Schriften, Reden, und Briefe von Julius Leber* (Berlin-Schöneberg and Frankfort on the Main: Mosaik-Verlag, 1952), pp. 280–281; Wilhelm Treue, *Deutsche Parteiprogramme seit 1861*, 4th ed. (Göttingen: Musterschmidt-Verlag, 1968), pp. 116–119; *Spiegelbild einer Verschwörung: Die Kaltenbrunner-Berichte an Bormann und Hitler über das Attentat vom 20. Juli 1944: Geheime Dokumente aus dem ehemaligen Reichssicherheitshauptamt* (Stuttgart: Seewald, 1961), pp. 206, 211–212, 233–235, 264, 315–317, 364, 415, 468, 499–501; Otto John, *Twice through the Lines* (London: Macmillan, 1972), pp. 57, 104, 138–139; Joachim G. Leithäuser, *Wilhelm Leuschner: Ein Leben für die Republik* (Cologne: Bund-Verlag, 1962), p. 248.

3. See Ger van Roon, *Neuordnung im Widerstand: Der Kreisauer Kreis*

innerhalb der deutschen Widerstandsbewegung (Munich: R. Oldenbourg, 1967), abridged in English as *German Resistance to Hitler* (London: Van Nostrand Reinhold, 1971); Theodor Steltzer, *Sechzig Jahre Zeitgenosse* (Munich: List, 1966); Hans Mommsen, "Social Views and Constitutional Plans of the Resistance," in Hermann Graml et al., *The German Resistance to Hitler* (London: Batsford, 1970); Michael Balfour and Julian Frisby, *Helmuth von Moltke: A Leader against Hitler* (London and Basingstoke: Macmillan, 1972).

4. Balfour and Frisby, p. 193.

5. See Gerhard Ritter, *Carl Goerdeler und die deutsche Widerstandsbewegung*, 4th ed. (Stuttgart: Deutsche Verlags-Anstalt, 1984), abridged in English as *The German Resistance: Carl Goerdeler's Struggle against Tyranny* (London: George Allen and Unwin, 1958); Goerdeler's papers, Bundesarchiv, Koblenz, Germany (hereafter BA).

6. Ulrich von Hassell, *The von Hassell Diaries, 1938–1944* (London: Hamish Hamilton, 1948); Hans Rothfels, *The German Opposition to Hitler* (Hinsdale, Ill.: Henry Regnery, 1948), pp. 99–101; Mommsen, "Social Views."

7. Hassell.

8. Ulrich von Hassell, *Vom andern Deutschland* (Zurich: Atlantis, 1946), pp. 386–396; Mommsen, "Social Views."

9. *Spiegelbild*, pp. 447–457.

10. See Eberhard Zeller, *Geist der Freiheit: Der zwanzigste Juli*, 5th ed. (Munich: Gotthold Müller, 1965), pp. 253–255, 489–490; Eberhard Zeller, *The Flame of Freedom: The German Struggle against Hitler* (London: Oswald Wolff, 1967), pp. 195–197, 395–396; *Spiegelbild*, pp. 191–192, 205–206, 226, 230–233, 258, 435–438, 447–448, 450, 453, 456, 465, 535.

6. Military Involvement

1. Chamberlain to Halifax 19 Aug. 1938, *DBFP*, 3rd ser., vol. 2 (1949), p. 686.

2. See Weber.

3. Helmut Heiber, ed., *Hitlers Lagebesprechungen: Die Protokollfragmente seiner militärischen Konferenzen, 1942–1945* (Stuttgart: Deutsche Verlags-Anstalt, 1962), pp. 587–588; National Archives, Washington, D.C., T-84 roll 175 frames 1544124-5.

4. See "Deutsche Gespräche über das Recht zum Widerstand," in *Vollmacht des Gewissens, vol. 1*, ed. Europäische Publikation e.V. (Frankfort on the Main, Berlin: Alfred Metzner, 1960), pp. 13–136; Walter Künneth, "Die evangelisch-lutherische Theologie und das Widerstandsrecht," ibid., pp. 166–176; Max Pribilla, "Der Eid nach der Lehre der katholischen Moraltheologie," ibid., pp. 161–165; Hermann Weinkauff, "Die Militäropposition gegen Hitler und das Widerstandsrecht," ibid., pp. 139–160; H. Kraus, ed., *Die im Braunschweiger Remerprozess erstatteten moraltheologischen und historischen Gutachten nebst Urteil* (Hamburg: Girardet, 1953).

5. Wolfgang Foerster, *Generaloberst Ludwig Beck: Sein Kampf gegen den Krieg* (Munich: Isar, 1953), pp. 9–29; Wolf Keilig, *Das deutsche Heer, 1939–1945: Gliederung—Einsatz—Stellenbesetzung* (Bad Nauheim: Verlag Hans-Henning Podzun, 1956–1970), p. 211/18; Ludwig Beck, *Studien,* ed. Hans Speidel (Stuttgart: K. F. Köhler, 1955), p. 18; Peter Hoffmann, "Ludwig Beck: Loyalty and Resistance," *Central European History* 14 (1981): 336–337.

6. *The Statesman's Year-Book: Statistical and Historical Annual of the States of the World for the Year 1934* (London: Macmillan, 1934), pp. 796, 873–878, 950, 1217–1218, 1260–1261, 1377.

7. Cf. Hoffmann, "Beck," p. 336.

8. Hoffmann, "Beck," pp. 338–350; Peter Hoffmann, "Generaloberst Ludwig Becks militärpolitisches Denken," *Historische Zeitschrift* 234 (1982): 120–121; N. H. Gibbs, *Grand Strategy, Vol. 1: Rearmament Policy* (London: HMSO, 1976), pp. 642–648.

9. Beck, p. 118.

10. *DGFP* D, vol. 1, no. 19, pp. 29–39.

11. Beck's notes of 12 Nov. 1937, Bundesarchiv/Militärarchiv, Freiburg i. Br. (hereafter BA/MA) N 28/4; cf. Beck's notes of 26 June 1935, BA/MA N 28/2; Nicholas Reynolds, *Treason Was No Crime: Ludwig Beck, Chief of the German General Staff* (London: William Kimber, 1976), pp. 100–102; Foerster, p. 55; cf. Hoffmann, "Beck," p. 338n31.

12. Hoffmann, "Beck," p. 338.

13. See *DGFP* D, vol. 1, no. 19, pp. 29–39; Deutsch, *Hitler and His Generals.*

14. Rönnefarth and Euler, pp. 40–49; Eduard Heilfron, ed., *Die Deutsche Nationalversammlung im Jahre 1919 in ihrer Arbeit für den Aufbau des neuen deutschen Volksstaates* (Berlin: Norddeutsche Buchdruckerei und Verlagsanstalt, 1920), II, 253; IV, 2096, 2652, 2668; VII, 79–80; VIII, 319.

15. Beck's memorandum of 20 May 1937, BA/MA N 28/2; cf. Müller, *Heer,* p. 235; Keitel, *Trial,* vol. 10 (1947), pp. 504–505; Wilhelm Keitel, *Generalfeldmarschall Keitel: Verbrecher oder Offizier? Erinnerungen, Briefe, Dokumente des Chefs OKW,* ed. Walter Görlitz (Göttingen, Berlin, and Frankfort on the Main: Musterschmidt, 1961) pp. 95, 178.

16. Hoffmann, "Beck," pp. 340–41.

17. Hoffmann, "Beck," pp. 337–339.

18. *Trial,* vol. 34 (1949), pp. 745–747; *ADAP* D, vol. 7, pp. 547–551; Colonel Jodl's Diary, *Trial,* vol. 28 (1948), pp. 355–356.

19. See *Trial,* vol. 25 (1947), pp. 414–427, 433–439; *Trial,* X, 508–509; Beck's ms. notes, BA/MA N 28/3; Keitel, *Verbrecher,* pp. 182–185; Gerhard Engel, *Heeresadjutant bei Hitler, 1938–1943,* ed. Hildegard von Kotze (Stuttgart: Deutsche Verlags-Anstalt, 1974), pp. 24–25; Foerster, pp. 99–106; Müller, *Heer,* pp. 300–309.

20. Hoffmann, "Becks militärpolitisches Denken," pp. 115–117; Edgar

Röhricht, *Pflicht und Gewissen: Erinnerungen eines deutschen Generals, 1932 bis 1944* (Stuttgart: W. Kohlhammer, 1965), pp. 120–123.

21. See Beck's ms. notes and drafts, BA/MA N 28/4; Müller, *Beck,* pp. 542–554; Gert Buchheit, *Ludwig Beck, ein preussischer General* (Munich: Paul List, 1964), pp. 147–152; Foerster, pp. 116–121; Müller, *Heer,* pp. 317–321.

22. *Trial,* XX, 624.

23. Beck's minute of 19 July 1938, BA/MA N 28/4; Müller, *Beck,* pp. 554–556.

24. Beck's ms. notes, BA/MA N 28/4; Müller, *Beck,* pp. 557–560.

25. Foerster, pp. 127–128; Helmut Krausnick, "Vorgeschichte und Beginn des militärischen Widerstandes gegen Hitler," *Vollmacht,* pp. 320–321; cf. Müller, *Heer,* pp. 326–332.

26. Beck's draft, BA/MA N 28/4; Müller, *Beck,* pp. 562–579; Foerster, pp. 128–137; Müller, *Heer,* pp. 333–338; cf. Hoffmann, p. 78.

27. Müller, *Heer,* pp. 333–338.

28. Major-General Curt Bernard, account dated 28 May 1945, typescript, IfZ ED 106 vol. 90; Foerster, p. 141; Brauchitsch during the Nürnberg Trial, *Trial,* XX, 569; Müller, *Heer,* p. 337.

29. *Trial,* XXVIII, 373–374; *Trial,* vol. 15 (1948), p. 345.

30. National Archives T-973 roll 15 pages 344–351; cf. Hoffmann, "Becks militärpolitisches Denken," pp. 117–118.

31. Friedrich Hossbach, *Zwischen Wehrmacht und Hitler, 1934–1938,* 2nd ed. (Göttingen: Vandenhoeck & Ruprecht, 1965), pp. 129–130.

32. Hoffmann, *History,* pp. 60–62.

33. Hans von Herwarth, *Against Two Evils* (New York: Rawson, Wade, 1981), pp. 123–135; Herwarth, letter to the author, 18 Dec. 1983.

34. Krausnick, "Vorgeschichte," pp. 341–342; Franz Halder, *Kriegstagebuch,* vol. 3 (Stuttgart: W. Kohlhammer, 1964), p. 534.

7. Failed Conspiracies

1. Hjalmar Schacht in "Protokoll aus der Verhandlung Halder, Spruchkammer X München," 15–21 Sept. 1948, mimeo. typescript, p. 121, BA/MA H 92-1/3; Hans Bernd Gisevius, *To the Bitter End* (Boston: Houghton Mifflin, 1947), p. 287.

2. Gisevius, *End,* pp. 306–307, 315–316; Gisevius, *Trial,* vol. 12 (1947), p. 214; Hjalmar Schacht, *Account Settled* (London: Weidenfeld and Nicolson, 1949), pp. 255–256; Schacht, "Protokoll," pp. 121–122.

3. See Hoffmann, *History,* pp. 81–96; Peter Hoffmann, *Widerstand, Staatsstreich, Attentat: Der Kampf der Opposition gegen Hitler,* 4th rev. ed. (Munich and Zurich: Piper, 1985), pp. 109–129.

4. Hoffmann, *Widerstand,* p. 120.

5. *DBFP*, II, 615.

6. See Ritter.

7. Ritter, pp. 110–121, 124–126.

8. Hoffmann, *Resistance*, pp. 367–368.

9. Domarus, pp. 1377–1393; *DGFP* D, vol. 8 (1954), pp. 227–230; *Parliamentary Debates*, 5th ser., vol. 352 (Commons), 12 Oct. 1939, cols. 563–565.

10. Peter Ludlow, "Papst Pius XII., die britische Regierung, und die deutsche Opposition im Winter 1939/40," *VfZ* 22 (1974): 337.

11. Ludlow, p. 337.

12. Helmuth Groscurth, *Tagebücher eines Abwehroffiziers, 1938/1940* (Stuttgart: Deutsche Verlags-Anstalt, 1970), p. 236; Hassell, *Diaries*, p. 88; Franz Halder, *Kriegstagebuch*, vol. 1 (Stuttgart: W. Kohlhammer, 1962), p. 133.

13. Groscurth, p. 241.

14. Gisevius, *End*, pp. 292–296; Erich Kosthorst, *Die deutsche Opposition gegen Hitler zwischen Polen- und Frankreichfeldzug*, 3rd ed. (Bonn: Bundeszentrale für Heimatdienst, 1957), pp. 62–63.

8. Contacts Abroad

1. T. P. Conwell-Evans, *None So Blind: A Study of the Crisis Years, 1930–1939* (London: Harrison & Sons, 1947), pp. 91–92.

2. See Hoffmann, *History*, pp. 547–548; Herwarth, pp. 122–125; Herwarth, letter to the author, 18 Dec. 1983; Hoffmann, "Beck," pp. 332–350; Hoffmann, "Beck's militärpolitisches Denken," pp. 101–121.

3. *ADAP* D, VII, 228–229.

4. See Hoffmann, *History*, pp. 99–110; intelligence report on a conversation between Goerdeler and Frank Ashton-Gwatkin, Brit. Foreign Office, dated 29 Aug. 1939, Public Record Office, London (hereafter PRO), C12878/15/18, FO 371/2298/1; Gibbs, pp. 689–714.

5. Hoffmann, *History*, pp. 170–171; Beus; Thun-Hohenstein.

6. Ludlow, p. 337.

7. Halder, *Kriegstagebuch*, I, 245; Hoffmann, *History*, pp. 167, 588.

8. PRO FO 371/26542/[C610], FO 371/26543/C10855, PREMIER 4/100/8; cf. Hoffmann, "Peace," pp. 11–12.

9. Hoffmann, *History*, pp. 205–210.

10. Hassell, *Diaries*, pp. 176–177.

11. James Douglas-Hamilton, *Motive for a Mission* (London, Basingstoke: Macmillan, 1971), pp. 156–157.

12. Hoffmann, "Peace," pp. 28–30.

13. Dietrich Bonhoeffer, *Gesammelte Schriften*, vol. 1 (Munich: Chr. Kaiser, 1958), p. 320; Bethge, *Bonhoeffer* (German ed.), pp. 732–737.

14. Bethge, *Bonhoeffer* (Engl. ed.), p. 648; (German ed.) p. 834; Willem Visser 't Hooft, *Die Welt war meine Gemeinde* (Munich: R. Piper, 1972), pp. 185–186; Professor Arvid Brodersen, interview with the author, 13 Jan. 1985; Bethge, *Bonhoeffer* (German ed.), pp. 855–858.

15. Hoffmann, *History*, pp. 216–224.

16. Hoffmann, *History*, pp. 228–234.

17. Balfour and Frisby, pp. 184–186.

18. Roon, *Neuordnung*, pp. 582–586; Balfour and Frisby, pp. 271–277; Hoffmann, *History*, pp. 225–227; Forrest C. Pogue, *United States Army in World War II: The European Theater of Operations: The Supreme Command* (Washington, D.C.: Office of the Chief of Military History, Department of the Army, 1954), pp. 102–106, 339–343; John Ehrman, *Grand Strategy*, vol. 5: *August 1943–September 1944* (London: HMSO, 1956), pp. 8–10, 110, 389.

19. Balfour and Frisby, pp. 295, 330.

20. Allen Welsh Dulles, *Germany's Underground* (New York: Macmillan, 1947), pp. 142–146; Jacob Wallenberg, interview with the author, 16 Sept. 1977.

21. Carl Friedrich Goerdeler, draft plan dated 19/20 May 1943, BA Nl. Goerdeler 23; Dulles, *Underground*, pp. 144–145.

22. *Spiegelbild*, pp. 410–412; Carl Friedrich Goerdeler, "Unsere Idee," typescript carbon copy, n.p. (Nov. 1944), pp. 24–25, 33–40, BA Nl. Goerdeler 26; Hoffmann, *History*, pp. 608–609n11.

23. Hoffmann, *History*, pp. 235–239.

24. Hoffmann, *History*, pp. 246–248.

25. Eden's telegrams from Moscow to the Foreign Office in War Cabinet records, PRO, Cab 65/24; Anthony Eden, *The Memoirs of Anthony Eden, Earl of Avon: The Reckoning* (Boston: Houghton Mifflin, 1965), pp. 332–352.

26. Anthony Eden, War Cabinet, Western Frontiers of the U.S.S.R., W.P. (43) 438, 5 Oct. 1943, PRO Cab. 66/41; War Cabinet 137 (43), 8 Oct. 1943, PRO Cab. 65/36, and Confidential Annex, PRO Cab. 65/40; Anthony Eden, War Cabinet, Anglo-Czechoslovak Relations, W.P. (42) 280, 2 July 1942, PRO Cab. 66/26; Detlef Brandes, "Grossbritannien und die Exilregierungen Polens, der Tschechoslowakei und Jugoslawiens vom Kriegsbeginn bis zur Konferenz von Teheran," Habilitationsschrift, Freie Universität Berlin, 1984, pp. 352–359; *FRUS 1943*, vol. 1 (1963), p. 542; *FRUS: The Conferences at Malta and Yalta, 1945* (1955), pp. 612–616; Churchill in the House of Commons 22 Feb. 1944 in Winston S. Churchill, *His Complete Speeches, 1897–1963*, ed. Robert Rhodes James, vol. 7: *1943–1949* (New York and London: Chelsea House and R. R. Bowker, 1974), p. 6893. Of the Germans, 14.470 million were expelled and 2.02 million were murdered. Gerhard Reichling, *Die deutschen Vertriebenen in Zahlen* (Bonn: Kulturstiftung der deutschen Vertriebenen, 1986), p. 36.

27. *FRUS 1943*, I, 542; *FRUS: The Conferences at Malta and Yalta*, pp. 159–163, 612–616.

28. "United States No. 3 (1941), Joint Declaration by the President of the United States of America and Mr. Winston Churchill, representing His Majesty's Government in the United Kingdom Known as the Atlantic Charter, August 14 1941," *Accounts and Papers: Five Volumes*, (4.) *Colonies, East India, Law, Crime, Miscellaneous, State Papers: Session 21 November 1940–11 November 1941*, vol. 8 (London: HMSO, 1941), Cmd. 6321; also in *The Times*, late London ed., 15 Aug. 1941, p. 4; *FRUS 1941*, vol. 1 (1958), pp. 367–369.

29. War Cabinet 84 (41), 19 Aug. 1941, PRO Cab. 65/19; *Parliamentary Debates*, 5th ser., vol. 374, House of Commons, Official Report (London: HMSO, 1941), 9 Sept. 1941, cols. 67–68; *Parliamentary Debates*, 5th ser., vol. 376, House of Commons, Official Report (London: HMSO, 1942), 18 Nov. 1941, cols. 187–188; *Parliamentary Debates*, 5th ser., vol. 398, House of Commons, Official Report (London: HMSO, 1944), 22 March 1944, cols. 853–854.

30. Hassell, *Diaries*, pp. 189–190; Freya von Moltke, Michael Balfour, and Julian Frisby, *Helmuth James von Moltke, 1907–1945: Anwalt der Zukunft* (Stuttgart: Deutsche Verlags-Anstalt, 1975); Goerdeler, draft plan in BA Nl. Goerdeler 23; Goerdeler, "Unsere Idee," in BA Nl. Goerdeler 26; *Spiegelbild*, pp. 126–127, 410–412.

9. Assassination Attempts

1. See Hoffmann, *History*, pp. 251–259, 279–289, 301–311.

2. Peter Hoffmann, "Maurice Bavaud's Attempt to Assassinate Hitler in 1938," in George L. Mosse, ed., *Police Forces in History* (London: Sage Publications, 1975), pp. 173–204; Hoffmann, *Security*, pp. 102–105, 180–181, 264–265; Klaus Urner, *Der Schweizer Hitler-Attentäter* (Frauenfeld and Stuttgart: Huber, 1980); Niklaus Meienberg, *Es ist kalt in Brandenburg: Ein Hitler-Attentat* (Zurich: Limmat Verlag Genossenschaft, 1980).

3. Anton Hoch, "Das Attentat auf Hitler im Münchner Bürgerbräukeller 1939," *VfZ* 17 (1969): 383–413; Johann Georg Elser, *Autobiographie eines Attentäters*, ed. Lothar Gruchmann (Stuttgart: Deutsche Verlags-Anstalt, 1970); Hoffmann, *Security*, pp. 105–118.

4. Groscurth, pp. 222–223.

5. Hoffmann, *Security*, p. 145; Hoffmann, *History*, p. 259; Hans Baur, *Hitler's Pilot* (London: Frederick Muller, 1958), pp. 114–115; Speer, pp. 170–172.

6. Walter Bussmann, "Politik und Kriegführung: Erlebte Geschichte und der Beruf des Historikers," *Fridericiana: Zeitschrift der Universität Karlsruhe*, no. 32 (1983), p. 10.

7. *Völkischer Beobachter*, Jan.–March 1943.

8. Scholl.

9. Erich von Manstein, personal war diary, Manstein's private papers in the possession of his son, Rüdiger von Manstein.

10. Philipp Freiherr von Boeselager (Kluge's aide de camp), interviews with the author, 21 Sept. 1983, 25 June 1984.

11. Hoffmann, *History*, pp. 281–283; Hoffmann, *Widerstand*, pp. 350–353.

12. Hoffmann, *History*, pp. 283–289.

13. Hoffmann, *Widerstand*, pp. 363–366; Gisevius, *End*, pp. 473–479.

14. Christian Müller, *Oberst i.G. Stauffenberg* (Düsseldorf: Droste, 1970), pp. 290–291.

15. Hoffmann, *History*, pp. 301–311.

16. Hoffmann, *History*, pp. 322–328.

17. Hoffmann, *History*, pp. 328–332.

18. Hoffmann, *History*, pp. 374–376.

19. Hoffmann, *History*, pp. 381–387.

20. See Hoffmann, *History*, chs. 41–46.

21. Peter Hoffmann, "Warum misslang das Attentat vom 20. Juli 1944?" *VfZ* 32 (1984): 441–462; Werner Vogel, interview with the author, 5 Sept. 1985.

22. Hoffmann, *History*, p. 412.

23. Hoffmann, *History*, p. 528.

Conclusion

1. Gisevius, *End*, pp. 551, 556.

2. Hoffmann, *Widerstand*, pp. 275–283.

3. Klaus-Jürgen Müller, *General Ludwig Beck* (Boppard on Rhine: Harald Boldt, 1980), p. 552.

4. Annedore Leber, *Conscience in Revolt* (London: Valentine, Mitchell, 1957), p. 140.

5. See Gerhard Taddey, ed., *Lexikon der deutschen Geschichte* (Stuttgart: Alfred Kröner, 1979), p. 1277; *10 Jahre Bundesrepublik Deutschland, 1949–1959* (Wiesbaden: Statistisches Bundesamt, 1959), pp. 31–32; *Statistisches Jahrbuch für die Bundesrepublik Deutschland, 1960* (Wiesbaden: Statistisches Bundesamt, 1960), pp. 78–79.

6. Hilberg, pp. 1201–1220.

7. Brigadier (ret.) Oskar-Alfred Berger, letters of 7 May and 30 June 1984 and interview of 12 July 1984.

8. *Spiegelbild*, pp. 110, 431, 443, 450, 471–474, 501, 520; *Prozess*, vol. 33 (1949), p. 424; Hans Rothfels, "Zwei aussenpolitische Memoranden der deutschen Opposition (Frühjahr 1942)," *VfZ* 5 (1957): 394; *Volksgerichtshof-Prozesse zum 20. Juli 1944: Transkripte von Tonbandfunden*

(Frankfort on the Main: Lautarchiv des Deutschen Rundfunks, 1961), pp. 100, 119; Balfour and Frisby, p. 218; Roon, *Neuordnung*, pp. 238, 245, 283, 326, 338–339; Ger van Roon, *Wilhelm Staehle: Ein Leben auf der Grenze, 1877–1945* (Munich: Gotthold Müller, 1969), p. 88; Hoffmann, *History*, pp. 324–325.

9. Balfour and Frisby, p. 218.

10. "Kriegstagebuch Nr. 1, Band Dezember 1941, des Oberkommandos der Heeresgruppe Mitte, geführt von Hauptmann d.R.z.V. Petersen," annex to p. 943, 9 Dec. 1941, IfZ.

11. Bethge, "Dietrich Bonhoeffer und die Juden," pp. 171–214; *The Holy Bible: Revised Standard Version Containing the Old and New Testaments* (New York: Oxford University Press, 1962), pp. 712–713.

12. Bethge, *Bonhoeffer* (Engl. ed.), pp. 649–654.

13. Schäfer, *Wurm*, pp. 156–171.

14. Benedicta Maria Kempner, *Priester vor Hitlers Tribunalen* (Gütersloh: Bertelsmann, Reinhard Mohn, n.d.), pp. 232–233.

15. Heiber, *Hitlers Lagesbesprechungen*, pp. 587–588; National Archives T-84 roll 175 fr. 1544124-5.

16. Wilhelm Scheid, "Gespräche mit Hitler (V): 'Freisler ist unser Wyschinski!' " *Echo der Woche*, 7 Oct. 1949, p. 5.

17. Trial films 3023-1 and 3179-2, BA, Film Archive.

18. BA/Film Archive Film no. 3179-I; Kurt Sendtner, "Die deutsche Militäropposition im ersten Kriegsjahr," *Vollmacht*, I, 438; Deutsch, *Conspiracy*, pp. 72–77.

19. *Trial*, XXXIII, 424.

20. Wagner, *Volksgerichtshof*, pp. 277–415; Bonhoeffer, I, 320; Bethge, *Bonhoeffer* (German ed.), pp. 732–737, 834, 855–585; (Engl. ed.), p. 648; Visser 't Hooft, pp. 185–186; Broderson, interview with the author, 13 Jan. 1985.

21. Balfour and Frisby, p. 186.

22. *Spiegelbild*, p. 507; Hoffmann, *History*, pp. 605–606.

23. Joachim Kramarz, *Stauffenberg: The Architect of the Famous July 20th Conspiracy to Assassinate Hitler* (New York: Macmillan, 1967), p. 185.

Index